TERRIAN JOURNALS'

HALF SERIOUS

(and wit)

by Donald Murray Anderson

Terrian Journals' Half Serious (and wit)
A Mythbreaker Book
First Edition
© Copyright 2022 by Donald Murray Anderson

ISBN 978-1-989593-28-8

For information address: mythbreaker@mail.com

Acknowledgement

Many inspirations from many different contexts and places catalyze the humour in this book, but the contents are completely out of my mind.

There are many old jokes that get bandied about and re-worked for generations. It's elder joke abuse? Someone is always saying or writing something funny.

Perhaps some of the old jokes inadvertently and deliberately stumble into these pages. They outlive and out laugh their authors.

Original comedic thought thus continues to defy and confound the whole misconception of unique and isolated intrahuman communications.

When jokes are spread and repeated, thanks are due to past speakers and writers whose eternal humour lives on in the mouths and volumes of their admirers and other parrots.

Out troduction

To spare readers the effort of using discretion or indiscretion, this volume of humour is not titled TJ JNG 2.

Besides, the jokes in TJ HS are much easier to understand, sometimes.

This is a volume of humourous and humourless anecdotes, puzzling over words, cheap shots, and wise cracks lacking in sagacity that defy readers to make nonsense of themselves and the world around you.

The humour and lack thereof reveal what makes me laugh and not laugh, sometimes simultaneously, in various spacial and temporal contexts.

Although I try to come up with titles to bring some order to this disorderly volume, the contents are definitely and indefinitely not in chronological or any other logical order.

I leave the false semblance of order in the unnatural domain of absolute rule bureaucrats in stiffened uniforms.

Jag reeling

The one time in my life that I'm admitted to a hospital, I'm not on the serious list. The doctor and nurses quickly realize that I can only be on the humorous list.

I create a very short column called "Weekly Wit" for a weekly newspaper. Readers soon realize that I'm half serious and half wit.

Winter in Ottawa is so frigid during the Cold War that the Soviet Embassy is flying the Hammer and Icicle.

This must be where ice cream, ice milk, and ice yoghurt are made.

Spring is arriving so my brain is no longer freezing. I don't need anti-freeze. Nor do I need uncle-freeze.

A brain drain is where thoughts and ideas find an exit and money replaces "home" sickness.

My grandparents send me a photograph of their "old faces". I write back asking, "How about sending a picture of your new faces?"

If I put my frying pan in cold water, will that give it steel distemper?

There's been a warm-cool wind blowing since early last night, gusting high sometimes, then disgusting.

In artesian areas, all is well.

A floating currency is more likely to sink than swim?

George took his dog to a flea circus and it stole the show.

What's asphyxiated? Heroins? Egypt was asphynxiated?

I visit another mine company's town up the valley. They tell me about improved rock hole silos. We all laugh when I realize they're saying raw coal silos.

At one time I'm thinking about raising dogs, but I can't figure out what to do with them once I get them into the air.

Being underground is just like being above ground, but darker. It's probably hardly noticeable at night.

It's the centennial of sound recording. Eat a record lunch.

Have you heard of a rock group called the conglomerates?

After the rock concert the performers left us all in the dust. Our senses were shattered, pulverized, and rolled.

People who read between the lines end up wearing bifocals.

I can summerize today's weather, but it's hot enough without my help.

Give me a home where the buffalo roam and I'll spend a lot of time cleaning the carpet.

I hear that the yacht factory is having a sail. Yacht dealers have sails clerks.

An English language student tells me he has an ice boat. Does it float? Is most of it below the surface? Oh, it's a nice boat!

Be sure to have an open mind, but close Sundays and holidays.

Does life without end also have no means?

Sorry you find the water fowl. At least there is no drought.

Is golf peripatetic?

I contact underworld figures today while taking 1000 ASA pictures of a new underground mining area: Panel 6.

Then I give the local RCMP mine tours. I mean mine not mine. I've heard of investigating underground organizations, but this is far-fetched.

I once believe that a think tank is an area for thtoring plumbing fixtures.

A newspaper add says that Guy Lombardo is playing in Lethbridge on October 11. I wonder what the final score will be. Should old acquaintances be forgotten?

Somebody at the office has his nose fixed, but he still smells the same. He's not as big of a fool as he used to be because he went on a diet.

Liver must be horse meat. Why else would hauses be kept in the livery stable?

Is the Grate Pumpkin just shredded pie in the sly?

Peanut farmers don't know how to cash in on peanut shells. That's the hull problem.

A woman at a party starts singing a lullaby that I have never heard before in a European language that I don't understand.

When she finishes I tell her that it's a song my mother sang at my bedside every night.

The singer says she didn't realize I was Polish. I say we were Shoe Polish, from Lower Slobia.

I'm using new stationary to write my letters. It's English. They call it James Bond. It's top secret. I can only write clearly on the bottom of each page.

The day is so mild that I decide to put my best foot forward and end up with a wet shoe.

Nuns of habit follow orders.

Play much cards? Fifty-two.

Some people say I'm a card. Others think I'm not dealing with a full deck. Those folks are real jokers.

Cards weren't played on the ark because Noah was standing on the deck.

The cheating card player was soon decked.

Word is a four-letter word. So is work.

It's not ready in black and white.

Giving a virtual address means indicating the next one.

Burmashavers of the world unite. You have nothing to lose but your beards.

I used to think irony was the opposite of permanent press.

Do cultured pearls come from oysters with degrees?

Is it true that mountain climbers spend their rest periods drinking steep tea?

The steel mine at Eagle Mountain, California is ironic.

Steel toe boots – Why would anyone do that?

Are hand laundries just for cowpokes?

The switchboard calls me and says, "It's a long-distance from Oakland." I say, "It certainly is."

For the past two hundred years Beethoven has been decomposing.

I take part in the speed reading introductory course. They say "read with your hand."

I say, "I used to be literate but now I pick up every scrap of paper I see."

What do you get when you cross 50 pigs and 50 deer? One hundred sows'n'bucks.

I used to think a taxidermist was a skin care specialist for cab drivers.

As J. Edgar Hoover used to say, "Ya, but how do you clean a vacuum?" What would there be to clean?"

Beware of gifts boring Greeks.

Car parts companies must have farms here. Somebody on the radio is talking about bumper crops.

Is a crowbar a saloon for birds?

Is Medicine Hat for headaches?

You mean C.B. radios are from Cape Breton?

There's a bridge down the road. I ask someone where it goes. She says it goes to the other side.

Mines have their pitfalls.

Cobblers reboot people.

The town is so small that it has no chain restaurant. But who eats chains? I prefer anti-oxidants.

Duck Ling is an exotic Chinese bird?

I live in the wilderness so long that I start to think that a traffic jam is some kind of preserve.

I'm going to a generic store. It's not a shopping centre for old people. Instead of a sign board it has a blank wall.

Some people must find my joke-telling rare. They say it's not well done.

I keep happy by remembering that the opposite of woe is giddy-up.

People who tell corny jokes must have husky voices.

Some people get puzzled over jigsaws and angry over crosswords.

Is Shirley Temple for religious gatherings?

Many church-goers are natural supporters of metric units for recording the air temperature. For a long time they've been singing glorious in ex-celsius deo. (apologies to my Latin teacher)

I used to think that a steeplechase was a race to the church.

Considering that Latin was born in Italy, if Italian-Canadians aren't Latin Americans then who is?

A truck show is always rigged.

Are you losing interest in bank rates?

If all the world's a stage then who's driving and who's riding shotgun?

I thought Banana Daiquiri was a character in one of Dicken's books.

Where's Ma hat McGhandi?

There's a town so small that both city limits signs are on the same pole.

I ask a supermarket clerk where the spare ribs are and he says he's not a doctor.

Did Heckle replace Hide or vice versatile?

Does Mr. Hide eat fudge Jeckles?

They laughed at Chris Colon. Who were his writers?

Is ground hog a substitute for hamburger?

Did the Greeks used to sleep on pillars?

Some oysters are stuffed. They must over-eat.

News about nuclear weapons tests above ground do not include glowing accounts.

Put out of circulation means dismiss delivery personnel.

Poor circulation spells Gutenberg coronary demise.

A strike by Canadian government translators could delay the budget speech. Nobody will know what the finance minister is saying until it's too late.

...

Some bowlers are so quiet that you can't even hear a pin drop.

Tonight I discover that curling has its ups and downs, but my two falls didn't even leave a bruise.

I also find out what cooling your heals means, but it feels more like my toes. I start getting cold feet about the rinks, but mine wins so I'll be back on the ice.

I hope I don't lose my standing again.

Curling news remains on ice.

Another night, curling is almost a clean sweep, for the other team.

My cousins' visit is so close to Hallowe'en, but they're no pump kin.

At last my thesaurus is here. I was running out of puns.

I have no worries about acid rain. The acid snow is what concerns me.

Maybe this phenomenon accounts for the holes in my clothes and socks?

Do Hangoosaram eat soul food?

I'm on a seafood diet. Every time I see food I eat it.

Bakers say making a cake is a stirring experience.

Why is there no macycle?

Recycling is a repeated ride an on old bike.

Attention Shoppers! The frozen food department may soon be having a whimsical sale.

What does Victor Hugo taste like? Misérable?

The temperance league offers anger management for insects?

Roomers

I gain free accommodation at a famous chain hotel in New York City where I'm attending a housing cooperative conference run by N.A.H.C.

One of the speakers at a panel discussion complains about the rooms, suggesting that we should all ask the hotel manager for bigger rooms.

She says the rooms are so small that the cockroaches are hunchbacked.

I don't see any roaches, but I do bang my tail bone on the edge of the bathroom sink because there is so little space between it and the toilet. I don't see a bruise.

Smorgasbord aboard

Mariko and I find Scandinavia and Suomi very expensive places to eat and sleep. The are second only to the U.K., which is the most expensive place we ever encounter.

Tokyo's reputation for high prices pales in comparison. That city is cheaper than the northernmost European countries, in our experience.

At the time of our first travels together, Paris and New York are cheaper too.

In Sverige it's very difficult for us to eat our usual well-balanced, nutritional diet. The very healthy bread, cheese, milk, and fruit take up most of our budget.

Then we make a discovery aboard a train: hot boiled water and cups. This enables us to add vegetables to our daily regime. We call them Swedish food.

For us that means buying packages of frozen mixed vegetables, emptying servings of them into cups, pouring the hot water over them, and then eating the resulting cup of fresh-tasting vegetables.

Deep purple

Is my skin turning mauve.
No. Why?
I've stayed in so many Auberge that I thought I was turning into an aubergine.

"Scotty. Beam me aboard." Make it oak.
It's autumn. Leaves are on the way out. Buy branches if you invest.

Every autumn the Muskoka forest turns over a new leaf.

Wind storm blows away colour leaf crop - news at 11.

There are so many women working at The Herald-Gazette newspaper that we may have to rename it The Harriet-Gazette.

I used to think Georgian Bay was either a type of horse, window, or department store.

The earth has a flat. Send out a celestial mechanic.

Thank goodness for the Hungarians. Only through their great discovery – the goulash, am I able to stay afoot on slippery surfaces.

Anyone wanting to create a slush fund could hardly pick a better day of weather for it.

If the Soviets invade Poeland, due to Solidarity, they better watch out for ravin's.

I tell an architect planning a university to keep the library and dining room well apart to discourage book worms.

How cheap are you? I'm so cheap that people think I'm a robbin'.

Psychoceramics are split dishes.

Psychocondriacs can't decide which pill to take first.

Psychodelic is a ready-to-eat food place serving customers who split their bills.

A racist is a malignant tumour.

Hatchets have accents.

King Kong's brother is Hong.

Xiang Giang is a street association with unfamiliar pronounciation.

Comic relief describes a joker on welfare.

It's easy to find a niche in life. In fact you can find many niche, sometimes simultaneously. Just look into the trees.

No kick

I used to go to events and parties where people did nicotine and alcohol, but it was never truly any fun for me. Inhaling toxic fumes and tolerating drunks never appeals to me.

But I manage to surprise people who know that I don't do any drugs, including caffeine, despite an occasional hit of cocoa.

They find me very "drunk' due to my humorous actions and words. It's easy to make inebriated people laugh about nothing.

I later conclude that's why nightclubs featuring standup comedians serve alcohol. After a few drinks, many people will laugh at anything.

An Amsterdam marijuana café would help even the worst joke tellers to establish a successful career. One deep breath of cannabis and the audience laughs and laughs.

When everything is funny we are all the kings of comedy.

I add humour to my personal drugless lifestyle whenever a woman attracting me for some reason tries to make herself seem less open-minded and unintelligent by asking me why I don't do social drugs.

I respond by breaking into song, "I get no kick from cham-paigne. Mere alcohol doesn't thrill me at all. But I get a kick out of you."

I sing the last sentence of the lyrics while pointing at the person asking the question.

Garden misjudging

My dad laughs when I tell him that I'm selected as a judge for a garden contest. Of course. I have no interest in or knowledge of gardening.

This makes me a perfectly impartial judge?

I know the tall thin green things are grass. Anything that's a different shape and colour is a flower, except bushes and trees.

Landscaping is all the stuff in one place.

Fortunately I'm only one of four judges. The others are the Mayor, Reg along with Tony and Loris from the land reclamation department of a mining company.

Gardeners get 10 points per item, but with five items per category – lawns, flowers, and landscaping.

Reg says 7. Loris says 8. I say 7.5. Or Reg says is this a 7.5 or an 8? I say, "Yes." Mayor Reg says he's the only non-politician judge in the group.

Nine hours of judging over three days enables us to decide twelve winners. There are many well-kept gardens in this town. At least that's what the other judges tell me.

Within a year and a half of my judging experience I'm taking a landscape architecture course at Ryerson, then Polytechnical Institute. Too late for my previous town.

I enjoy the course and do well in it, but I don't complete it due to a diversion that takes my attention away from my studies. Her name is...

So I'm now incompletely qualified to judge a garden contest.

Help call

I need to hear you right away;
Please phone me now, without delay.
I cannot wait another day:
So, governor, please make my stay.

Intell

Sometimes talking to yourself is the only means of participating in an intelligent conversation.

Do You Speak Curling?

Curl Canada may have to start offering degrees in linguistics when the organization begins the season with a one-day instructional clinic at my club.

Perhaps Curl Canada will help other new curlers avoid my semantic problems as a new curler.

The first time I step onto a curling rink, in a mining town, I'm swept off my feet.

The doctor says nothing is broken and the pain at the base of my spine is gone a few weeks later.

Undaunted by my first experience, I come back to the ice enthusiastic and join a Toronto club last fall, two years after my first fall.

When the club hands me a broom, I think they're hiring me to clean up the place.

Someone at the other end of the ice starts yelling, "Sweep!"

That makes me decide I don't want the job. Who wants a bossy supervisor anyway?

So I decide to learn how to curl instead.

Learning the game means learning a whole new language.

Experienced curlers should remember that they're dealing with aliens, even if some of us have Scottish-sounding names like mine, and help the newcomer learn the language as well as the moves of curling.

I remember the first time someone tells me to shoot a rock. I tell him that I would first need some kind of weapon.

Some of the old-timers suggest that I start out with draw curling. So I sit down and began sketching blue and red circles.

The whole team gets mad for some reason, saying I'm holding up the game.

My problems are just beginning. I find it hard to respond to phrases like, "The skip gave him too much ice."

Why does everybody have to talk about the bar service during the game?

I'm told to put a rock in the house. I think he means I should take a rock home for practice.

But it's so heavy that I can't even get the thing out to the street. Then some wise guy tells me to put the rock through the house.

I think mixed curling is for me. I think it will help me become less mixed up about the sport.

The first thing I do is slide down the ice to ask a beautiful woman if she would go out to dinner with me.

By the time I'm halfway down the ice she's already shouting, "Yes! Yes!" Curlers must be mind-readers.

The first instructions I receive have something to do with medicine and attendance. I guess new curlers are accident prone. There's talk about interns.

They must be club members working as doctors.

There's also talk about out-turns, a backward form of turn-outs I suppose.

There's also some strange talk about turning the rock to ten o'clock. But I've never heard of any games starting after nine.

Or is that about the old song, "Rock around the clock"?

From what I'm told at this first informal lesson, I gather that the basic goal of the game is not to play at all.

The team I'm assigned to tells me that when I'm good enough I can skip it.

My puzzlement increases.

Part of the essential equipment of this sport is a slider. I see a lot of sliders. I'm surprised none of them fall down.

Fortunately, despite all my difficulties learning the curling language during lessons, I learn a few things before starting the game.

Some people at my club probably don't realize how little I really know when I talk about the Brier.

When I'm a child, I thoroughly enjoy all those stories about Brier Rabbit and Brier Bear.

Also, I find out what a bye is at an early age. Later I discover a bye is also quite common in Newfoundland and at shopping centres everywhere.

Despite this knowledge, and the accompanying ability to make the experienced curler think I know more than I really do, there are still a number of matters which are beyond me.

For instance, why in the world would anyone curl for a silver broom? The straw ones seem to be a lot more durable and easier to handle.

I do understand the utility of a bon spiel. Although I think some curlers go a bit too far when they try to tell me that people burn rocks.

Rocks may crack, but they cannot burn on ice.

Bon spiel champions at my club tend to be insurance agents and bankers. They use good lines all the time when they talk about their games.

So do I. Every new curler needs a bon spiel to explain away bad shots, and to compensate for a lack of knowledge of the curling language.

Comprenez? Curling is a game full of vices; takes seconds; both men and women can lead; and you can skip it.

I-kido-you-nought

When Mariko and one of her Aikido friends are among people not involved in the martial art, I suggest they give a demonstration of eye-key-dough.

I always need a good joke.

I will say random Japanese words and they can act them out as if they were Aikido techniques.

I would call out, "Onagaishimasu", at which point they could go down on their knees and make begging motions.

When I say, "Onigiri" they could put their palms together as if applauding softly to each other.

"Omiyagi" would elicit generous gestures between them.

"Oshogatsu" would prompt them to act out offering each other a great variety of food and beveridges.

"Isogashi" would involve them moving away from each other in every direction while ignoring one another.

"Ishoni" would consist of handshakes and hugs.

If I say, "Tokidoki" they could hold up their legs, jingle key chains, point at their feet, and give thumbs up signs. That would be bilingual (English/Japanese) Aikido.

Saying, "O mizu" would tell them to jump very high in the air and come back to the group curled up in a roundish shap many times in a row.

"Omocha" would signal that they should roll on the floor, do some doll-like pantomine, and march like the Rockettes in uniform at their Christmas show.

The finale or end would be "Oshiri", which would be bottoms up in whatever manner the demonstrators wish to portray that.

This would fascinate and tantalize people unfamiliar with martial arts and set back understanding of Aikido at least a hundred years.

If everyone in Toronto had a sore throat would that make it ah... one hoarse town?

Vancouver spell hurts Toronto

The Vancouver-like winter conditions [now plaguing] Toronto are more than a southern Ontario person can stand.

Forget those pretty Ontario winter scene calendar pictures.

The usual outdoor skating, snowballs, and cross-country skiing that make a Toronto winter bearable are painfully absent.

This urban bastion of Canadian winter, home of the happy ice seekers, is becoming just another mud city in the rain.

Burrard Inlet blues spare no one in Toronto. That Vancouver loom and gloom of clouds is invading the lakeshore and psyche of Toronto.

A burst of sunlight is now a festival. People spend entire days in dullness, pretending they are trapped in the dark, underground subway tunnels of T.O.

The Van blands of winter are too much for the average T.O. person to handle.

Cold, snow, and ice seem like comforting normalcy compared with the cataclysm of a mild Ontario winter.

Lost ice skaters wander the parks, starring and straining their over-thawed eyes for some sign of hard winter.

The Toronto mayor could yet declare a state of emergency.

Ontario Provincial Police would then be able to deliver the provincial emergency stockpile of dry ice, which might be the only salvation for the south Ontario snow-flake-harvesting industries.

The ploughs have gone silent from a drought of real winter conditions.

Great Lakes shipping channels, already seriously thawed out, could be quickly refrozen by freighters loaded with relief snow supplies from the benevolent people of Baffin Island.

Migratory birds threatening to return and create an uneasy atmosphere of early spring, would be collected, caged, and flown back to Florida under guard, in military cargo planes.

The unthinkable would be stopped short. Toronto would not have to contend with the terrifying sight of flowers blooming or buds budding in the wintertime.

An end would be put to those growing rumours that émigrés from B.C. have been smuggling in warm temperatures.

The panic of an acute umbrella shortage in Toronto would quickly be brought to an end. Empty snowsuits would no longer be found deserted on doorsteps and in back alleys.

Toronto's ultimate fate will depend upon the final departure of the overwhelming Vancouver-like winter conditions of recent weeks.

Off the hook

Off line over & out

My office phone at Dentonia Park Cooperative Homes rings too often. It's a distraction.

There are suggestions that it needs an answering machine.

When my boss Shirley phones I say, "I told you never to call me at the office." She bursts out laughing.

I write a notice saying that if the phone rings and there's no answer it means I'm working. If it's busy, I'm not here.

I begin to keep a phone log to report calls and how I handle them.

Dentonia is a very good-humoured community, so I can write the log in an interesting way and add a bogus version to make Dentonians laugh.

Here are some excerpts from actual and untrue phone calls:

April 1: 9:45 a.m.: Toni wants info from her house, in exchange for cookies.

April 2: 4:00 p.m.: Lantana phoned to make a nuisance of themselves (again).

April 3: 10:42: Noorali wants to know if the city is picking up garbage as usual on (Good) Friday. – Well, uh, gee, uh, beats me. I just throw it down the chute where I live.

12:21 noon: Toni calls to tell me she's wunning off wabbits.
3:16 p.m.: Sandra phones to find out Neill-Wycik's new phone number. How should I know? I just live there. Did the old number die?

April 8: 1:05 p.m.: Acting President Sandra phones to make sure that all is well during the absence of President James I. (No coup d'etat is anticipated.)

April 9: Shirley leaves agenda item for corporate secretary – I miss the noon radio news lead story, again! No wonder I don't know what's going on in the world.

April 14: 1:44 p.m.: Magazine subscription service – she had a great voice - gave a spiel.

April 15: 12:10 noon: Shirley calls for assorted matters. 12:20: Shirley calls to keep me from eating lunch.

12:34: Shirley – more of same.

1:57 p.m.: Cheryl M. is sending Miriam and David courier with fry pan to have handle removed.

April 24: 10:12 a.m.: Jean S. suggests who to call for missing keys. 11:32: Louise J. reports on key mystery. 11:34: Betty Mc. Solves the mystery of the missing keys. 11:58: Larry of Grindstone wants to know... (Why can't I listen to the noon news on the radio?) 12:37 p.m.: Toni calls about the mango shake.

April 28: 11:07 a.m.: Hardware store wants Shirley, won't say why, leaves phone number – very intriguing. Could be a clou. 11:11: Dentonia Daycare inquiry (wrong number); Who am I – W.C. Fields? 11:46: A four bedroom apartment "buyer" phones. I sell him Main St. Bridge. 11:51: A wrong number returning my call. No kidding. 12:42 noon: Louise C. wants parking space - I "Kookie" Burns the jalopy Dad, - crazy, cool cat that I am.

April 29: 10:36 a.m.: two bedroom request – hum a few bars...12:03 noon: Donna B. wants her maintenance cheque and to get married. Sorry, I'm busy. 12:12: Louise C. doesn't want "to slap around Jim" Mu. for a parking space.

12:26 Louise J. says her door is open and I can come over any time. She wants to help me form a co-op in California. How many people can I get into a bachelor apartment?

April 30: 10:38 a.m.: Toni says I should wait longer when I ring a door bell. 11:14: Jean S. wants garbage bags. 11:44: Hardware store wants Shirley.

Communications jam

In an era of highly competitive mixed communications media, the community television station announces the cancellation of "New Postage Stamps".

During an ice storm depriving most people in New Brunswick of electricity for several days, N.B. Power reps are guests on still broadcasting radio stations.

Using a battery-powered radio receiver, I hear the reps saying, "If you want to know which areas are without power, go to our website."

N.B. Power sends me a very indignant and defensive reply when I complain about how silly it is to tell people without electricity to use their electrically-run computer devices to go to a website for power outage information.

If people have any power at all, it's devoted to lights, keeping perishable food from spoiling, and listening to the radio to find out which areas are without power.

Honest Framer Replaces Post Office

An honest picture framer can sometimes pick up where the post office drops off.

Franz Ehlebracht and his wife, proprietors of New Style Picture Framing, 1584 Bloor Street West, are the honest framers.

They're walking by Indian Trail on Wednesday afternoon and find a soggy box lying against the curb, about to be covered by a snowfall.

The box is a parcel. It's mailed from Vancouver to an address on Howard Park Avenue.

The Ehlebrachts carry the box to their shop, look up the person who's supposed to receive the parcel, and phone him.

The parcel's rightful owner finds the jogging suit and jar of jam inside the box unharmed by the post office random curb delivery service. Only the cookies are crumbled.

It's amazing that the Ehlebrachts can phone me. I don't have a phone connected in my attic apartment for a long time.

My last access to a phone in Toronto is someone else's at Neill-Wycik, if you don't count the free one in the hallway of Hart House and at my work station at the architecture library.

Just Me & My Phone

I quit my phoning habit more than five months ago. Then, without warning, I finally break, and ....

Little do I realize the gamble I'm taking by plugging in that rather innocuous looking dumbell on a fat roulette wheel.

Despite my very innocent and romantic motivation to rejoin the land of dial tones and busy signals – la Belle vie, the results are startling.

The first night we spend together, my little black dialer rings me awake at 2:20 a.m. So long without a ring, my head doesn't recognize this intruding sound.

But only one person knows my number. Surely that person would not pull such a prank.

I raise the dumbell to my ear. Blank. Oh no, a random caller! How bizarre! Then - "Is Vera there?"

The next day I tell a few friends they can finally reach me. In return I get three calls.

One is a poll about smoking. I don't smoke.

Then another pollster asks me who I would vote for in a provincial election.

The third call is for some business I've never heard of.

Later, a stereo shop calls to ask when "Mrs. Anderson" would be home. I reply, "As soon as I get married". I could add: "to a very conservative woman.".

Apparently the shop thinks it has a way of seeing into my future.

You see, Mrs. Anderson owes $25 on a colour television set. Please pay up, wherever you are Mrs. A. I can't accept a wife without a good credit rating.

Also, if I end up paying the $25, I would at least like to have a look at the set. I have no colour television at my place.

The excitement in my life increases dramatically.

Not only do I have the surprise and wonder of wrong phone numbers, I gain the soapbox experience of being able to express my opinions to pollsters and I learn who is not paying her bills.

I also join the multilingual and cosmopolitan elite of Toronto.

Callers speak to me in Italian, Ukrainian, Polish, and German.

What fascinating conversations we could have, if only I could say more than two words in each of these languages.

At last someone calls from Mississauga. He even has my correct phone number. Unfortunately, I don't know any of the Mississaugese language.

While I thrive on all this excitement, the strains and stresses are too much for my basic, standard phone.

My little dumbell fares poorly. It begins to wheeze, crackle, and hiss every time I pick it up to dial and talk. Soft words are no help.

Finally, the inevitable happens. My phone dies.

The poor thing must be the victim of a nervous breakdown. That cute little hum is no more.

I come home one evening, pick up the dumbell, and only hear the sound of my ear brushing against those tiny, empty holes.

I call the boys in blue overalls to pick up the remains.

To this day the experience haunts me. I wake up in the night and imagine I've just heard a faint ringing sound in my ears.

So, to all my friends who think they have my number – please – write me a letter.

Sorry, right number

My long-time Toronto friend has many phone numbers. She sends me all of them in an e-mail message. When I call one of them she says, "How did you get this number?"

I'm older than she is.

Self-incarceration

Touring an art gallery in what used to be a prison in Québec City, Mariko and I improve our vocabulary and understanding of the world around us.

In French, a cell bloc is called "bloc cellulaire". I joke with Mariko, saying that I wonder if they have téléphone cellulaire for prisoners too.

But there's a not so humourous link. No matter where a cellular phone user goes, s/he is always held prisoner by it.

A cellular phone is self-imprisoning by the user's choice.

It's also an employer's best friend, enabling him/her to capture the employeed anywhere and any time.

IT gives a whole new meaning to the terms permanent employee and lifelong employment. The sad fate of the employeed takes a turn for the worse.

Cell bound

To paraphrase the advertising for the first "Alien" movie: In Cyberia nobody notices anything.

We who aren't celled are invisible. So we can do anything?

I'm hoping to see a mime sitting in a subway car mocking the cell users around her/him.

I study the subway cell zombies because I'm exposed to them more often by my frequent rides.

Looking around me aboard the chikatetsu I see nobody who seems to know where s/he is, I mean his/her actual physical and geographical location.

S/he might only and occasionally become aware of the station we are approaching thanks to recorded announcements telling her/him. But only if s/he's listening.

It's easy to block out and ignore the announcements.

In some subway systems, when I'm thinking about something, including this writing, I sometimes miss my stop or get surprised by it at the last moment because I'm not paying attention to the station announcements.

I'm looking at one celled-up person sitting not far away. She's suddenly animated, looking alive and aware, quickly looking around her as if coming to life.

Her facial expression says she's discovering a world new to her.

Where am I? How did I get here?

I'm smiling and joking to myself. But it's no joke. She's realizing it's her stop and hopping out of the subway car like the White Rabbit in the book "Alice in Wonderland".

The new look!

Isolated in the lounge at Haneda Airport prior to quarantine, each time that I drowsily look around it seems as if most passengers are not sleeping.

They're hypnotized electronically, mainly by tiny, eye-straining, and cross-eye-inducing phones.

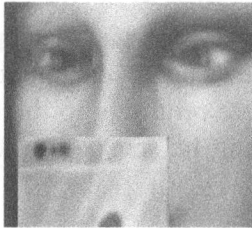

In their pseudo-wakefulness they're like "gamers" who sit at screens until they die.

This goes way beyond the toilet pot under Beethoven's piano. At least that LAB created something while staring at his ivory keyboard.

New face

In a Kazan Metro train we're sitting across from a very old-looking woman with a very puffy face and wrinkles etched into it like battle scars. It expresses pain.

Her features are moulded glum and grim with a pall of eternal and unalterable sadness.

Whispering together about our thoughts, ideas, and impressions of the moment, in one of our common mysterious foreign languages, Mariko suddenly lurches at my face and pecks it with a quick kiss.

The old woman's face melts dramatically into uncontrollable laughter. She shakes her head at me as if in teasing disapproval.

From this moment on she can't contain the humour breaking up her glum mask. I smile at her and she continues to burst with joy.

It seems to take her a very long time to contain herself.

Somehow she eventually manages to suppress all her mirth and all her facial muscles again, disciplining her laugh lines back into frowns before returning to the oblivion of ignoring us and recomposing herself before leaving us and the subway train.

But can she ever forget the long fit of happiness?

Unreal estate

Agencies selling property make great use of the portable telephone to sell you lair. Some agents are liars selling lairs to cell you up with a mortgage. It's a life sentence, regardless of period.

Schizophonic

After observing people with cell phones in various parts of the world talking to their invisible friends, sometimes with great emotion, I jokingly make a suggestion to my physically present friend Gillian from U.B.C.

I say that all schizofrenic people should be issued cellulaire phones so that they can blend in more easily while walking in the streets talking out loud to apparently no one.

Gillian calls it a great idea.

In the crazy world of cell phone use, why are only some people labelled mentally ill?

Addictive techo-pandemic

Cellular phone usage is so rampant that it goes well beyond the age when "everyone" does nicotine and alcohol and when owning a polluting vehicle is "essential".

In Canada, legalized marijuana drug sales are down. Cell users don't need it. They're cyberspaced out.

Crowning achievement

At UofT I like taking a break at Hart House, a very old building now serving as a student centre.

It has many quiet rooms for reading, a music listening room, a gym, a big dining hall, a cafeteria, and a free phone.

I take my bag lunches there. A noon jazz concert is coming up.

Meetings of the debating club also occur here. I attend some debates. At one the resolution is that Alberta Premier Peter Lougheed be coronated.

Usually, I only listen to the debates. But this one is so funny that I decide to speak. I decide to play the stereo-typical image of someone from Alberta.

Each speaker is introduced before saying a word. Instead of telling the person introducing speakers my name, I hand him my Alberta birth certificate.

He reads my name and says, "from Alberta".

There is a big pitcher of water for all speakers and I know exactly what I'm going to do with it.

Instead of taking one of the nearby glasses, I pick up the whole pitcher and, dramatically, pour water down my throat, spilling some over my clothes.

Perhaps somehow not understanding the joke I'm pulling, one of the moderators desperately tries to offer me a glass. But it's too late.

I wipe my mouth by rubbing it with a broad sweeping motion on my shirt sleeve. Then my opening words: "I'm from Alberta!" Uproar of laughter.

I explain that "Pete" Lougheed is not from the Alberta town of Coronation. I add that "Pete" is far too modest to ever accept the kingship.

That's about all I say. The moderators talk to me after-wards, saying they enjoy my contribution.

But, despite my humble efforts to influence the outcome of the debate, the resolution passes for crowning Pete.

Given what happens in the constitutional realm - I too want to crown him, in a different sense

K as in N

While studying at l'Université Laval in Québec Ciy, Mariko uses part of the university library that requires students to leave their student cards to use certain materials.

The librarian places the cards in a filing system according to the alphabetical order of students' family names, to make card retrieval easy.

But one day, when Mariko returns to the library desk for her card, the librarian tells her that there is no card bearing her family name.

The librarian is looking under K, for Marie Konishida. Apparently, the librarian files cards without looking carefully at them, giving the impression that she's illiterate.

A few words for Mariko

Similar sounds in Nihongo and Español amuse Mariko.

The vowels are similar. She already knows vaca and ajo. She adds to these mucha, which means too risky in Nihongo.

I tell her about an old U.S. cowboy movie star who is always asking Mexicans to take him to their "head honcho".

Mariko is amused to know that I think honcho is Español. Joncho?

Then we start converting Japanese words starting with "j" into their Español pronounciation. So Mariko almost sends a student to Hiromaru subway station instead of Jiromaru.

When I ask a bus driver if he goes to that station I have to think carefully about pronouncing the "j".

Then we start talking about U.S. singer Hennifer Lopez.

Curt Repurt

The S.P.C.A. files suit in an L.A. County Court against scientists professing the theory of evolution.

S.P.C.A. spokespersons say that apes are responsible for Ayatolah Komaniac and the Moribund Majority.

In a counter suit, the Moribund Majority contend that the evolution theory does have some substance, as evidence scientists professing the theory.

A split decision by the Banana Supreme Court finds both defendants offensive.

Having a belt, or not...

Is my money belt here or there? If it's there, please send it. Otherwise don't. Maybe its location is neither here nor there.

Film politics

The movie menu at The Revue Theatre on Roncesvalles Avenue starts with "Horse Feathers" and ends with "Duck Soup".

They must be left wing movies and all the stars are named Marx.

The middle of the evening feature is Ronald Reagan, starring in the epic film which helps make him what he is today, "Bedtime For Bonzo".

Jimmy Carter plays Bonzo. Bonzo wins.

The movie house is showing the triple feature almost on the eve of a U.S. presidential election.

I invite some of my Dentonia friends to a group viewing, using a political description of the event. It'll be a night of the next U.S. president versus the Marxists my invitation says.

I'm only joking about the presidential election prediction, but the jokes turns out to be on me and the U.S.

Later, during a visit to the U.S. capital city, I buy a "Bedtime For Bonzo" post card and write:

Well, just the other day, I was thinking that no one will ever make a monkey out of this president.

He only sets back the U.S. about thirty to fifty years.

In Touch
a sporty review of recreation jargon.

Okay sports fans, here's some norts spews that'll put the points back on your scoreboard:

Remember to keep your head down, chin up, arms and legs straight, bend your knees, and don't use your wrists. It's all in the ankles.

How often has someone said just that to you?

Well – times have changed. What's good for Bonzo is good for the nation. Let's win this one for the Gipper!

Yoga: The latest craze in contact sport seems to be yoga. The most popular variety contains honey and fresh fruit.

Off Track Betty: Whenever the duplicating machine doesn't print the newsletter properly, someone says it's off track.

Grey Cup: If somebody doesn't volunteer to help clean the coffee mugs after a party, everyone will be drinking out of grey cups next time.

Curling: It's a popular hair style lately.

Jogging: At some time in the future, someone reminds you about the volunteering you forgot to do.

Hookey Night In Canada: That's when someone doesn't show up for a meeting. It's very rare.

Hokey Night In Canada: That's when you end up at home some evening, reading corny stuff like this page.

Bow Ling: Often mistaken for a Chinese martial art, like Kung Fu, this sport is actually invented by the famous Irish pumpkin thrower: Jack O'Lantern.

Hocky Pool+1: For the second year in a row, some people are talking about a pool. How about a heated one?

Roller Skating: Someone brings an 8-wheel drive to the social committee.

Running: A poet-chef runs for office. Does this mean run-on sentences in poems and runny sauces in the cuisine?

Hunting: Your administrative committee is trying to track down stationery supplies that keep hiding in different homes. If you're game, please leave a trail to your door.

Bob Sledding: Our resident carpenter is building a wooden sleigh for the snow.

Cricket: a female creek?

Bask et ball: a Spanish separatist game?

Gym Nauseum: a place to go to figure out why there are so many people named Jim in my paternal family?

Sai Ling: an off shore martial art?

Boxing: something you'll be doing for Christmas?

Do coaches have play playwrites?

Are players in the field at half time or staccato?

Time out!

Seasoned Gratings

Twelve Days of Christmas - no longer for the birds

On the last day of Christmas my true love says to me,
"I have no…thing to put on your tree."

"On this last day of Christmas,
I wished to give to you…:
Seven swans a-swimming,
Six geese a-laying,
Four calling birds,
Three French hens,
Two turtle doves,
And a partridge in a pear tree!"

"But I can't offer to you,
gifts that are all now extinct,
All I <u>can</u> tell you is what's now in store."

"There'll be:

"More factory smoke,
New pesticides,
More toxic fumes,
and a hundred more years of bush wars."

"They all make toxic waste,
Poison water, soil, and air,
and kill all the bugs that birds eat,"

"Global warming resulting is heating up the air,
'til it's <u>too</u> hot for all birds to bear."

"Birds that can still survive all the toxins and the heat,
we'll <u>ne</u>ver be able to meet."

"There'll be

No wings a-waving,
as from the coup they flew,
they all died from the avian flu."

"I might search for a pear tree,
but that will be in vain,
They're all long gone now
from the acid rain."

On the last day of Christmas my true love says to me,

"There are no swans a-swimming,
No geese a laying,
No calling birds,
No French hens,
No turtle doves,
And no partridges and no pear trees.

If you don't like this swan song,
Then don't complain to me.
For a <u>bet</u>ter world change your life style.

Off White Christmas
(A White Christmas Update)

Stop dreaming of a white Christmas,
with every news report you see.
Artic ice is melting and crops are failing,
while dry <u>land</u> sinks under the seas.

For…get about a white Christmas,
folks would rather drive their cars.
Motor minds all idling, always declining,
 Breath..ing ex..haust fumes all day.

To really see a white Christmas,
climb to Sagamarta's peak,
Or move to the south pole and stay,
 and enjoy Antarctica that way.

If you still dream of white Christmas,
 then there's something you can do.
Wake up and start facing the facts,
Save the planet while you're still in tact..

You'd better watch out

You'd better watch out!
You'd better not joke!
You'd better not smile!
I'm telling you why.
Insecurity's stocking you.

I. T. knows where you're sleeping.
I. T. knows where you live.
I. T. knows all your bank accounts.
It can freeze your assets quick.
SO!

You'd better watch out!
You'd better not gripe!
Keep all your opinions just to yourself.
I. T.'s listening to you right now.

I. T. knows where you're going
I. T. knows where you've been.

I. T. knows who sits next to you.
So expect a random check!
WOE!

Just step over here
and raise your arms high.
You know the routine.
It's like a street crime.
Stand on your head and just salivate.

Start taking off your shoes now.
Next time we'll strip you down.
You must do everything we say.
You're completely in our power.
SO!

Don't get out of line
or show resistance!
Or you'll be inside
a tiny dark room
for interrogation right now!

With billy clubs and night sticks
a tazer zap or four!
We'll shock you into submission
if you try the exit door!
OW!

You'd better watch out!
Start watching your step.
We've got your mug shot and your fingerprints.
Al Capone has nothing on you!

I. T. says we're at war now
to fight for evermore.
I. T. has us all in its sights!

So be good for goodness sake!
WOE!

You'd better watch out!
Don't say what you think!
You're name will be on the terrorist list.
There'll be no more flying for you.
I. T. knows what you're reading.
I. T. knows what you watch.
I. T. knows when you do complain.
So, never say what you think.
SHH!

Now just remain calm
while standing in line.
Don't brush your teeth
or drink water here.
Redefining "freedom" is sweet.

How did this ever happen?
Remember human rights?
We're all becoming "Tramps" now,
like in Charlie Chaplin's flicks.
YIKES!

Good luck to us all
in this police state.
Insecurity's ever so bleek.
It's better to take risks in life.

What do we stand for
if we lose it all?
It's better to be free
than insecure.

Let's all take our chances.

Let's all take our chances.
Let's all take our chances again.

We're driving instead of Christmas

We're driving instead of Christmas.
We're driving instead of Christmas.
We're driving instead of eating.
Skipping three meals a day.

Good tidings to you
With trucks, cars, and vans.
Good tidings for a full tank
of petroleum fuel.

With no pie or plumy pudding,
With no pie or plumy pudding,
We cannot afford to buy them.
Shipping costs are too high.

No turkey or any trimmings,
No bread, corn, or butter cookies,
The bird flu and biofu-els,
have used up all supplies.

There's no food to eat at Christmas.
We have nothing in our stomachs.
We're driving instead of Christmas.
All the food's in gas tanks!

Wallowing In "First Word" Folly

Wallowing in "first world" follies,
Tra-la-la-la-la-la, la-la-la-la
Tis the season we call jolly,
'cause we are inside the "first world" club.

While we don straight gay apparel
Others toil in sweat shops making more.

As we count our money's measure,
They can only make a buck, or two, a day.

While we cringe and hide in panic,
They are maimed and killed by arms we sell.
As we drink to toast the season,
Potable water eludes them all.

We say they're all dumb and lazy,
While we play - all of our - on-line games.
"First world's" full of arms and money,
We do little good. We're impotent.

If you don't like "first world" follies,
and its global <u>min</u>ority rule,
Just permit the third world to lead.
Eighty per cent of hu..mans live there.

That'll be true, fair world order.
better than "first world's" apartheid rule.
If you don't like "first world" bullies,
start working for world democracy.

Icebergs?

An ice berg is a settlement beside a frozen body of water?

Out West
(where all the stars ain't on sherrif's chests)

Out west is a land where the cattle low and the wave's high. That much is true. But there's much more, and lots of misunderstanding about..... THE WEST.

Take it from me, I live out west.

I remember one time when I was way out west, on the edge of the lands of the Missassauga, near Islington.

An old timer on shank's mare stops a spell to chaw on some kaisers with me. He says something that I'll never forget:

"Son," (he's not my father), "what you call the west depends on how old you are. Some people call High Park the western frontier."

He's right. Many people spend a whole lifetime going no farther west than the College streetcar.

And yet, a lot of things are said about the west. For instance, some polls tell us that a separatist club is growing in the western provinces.

(There's great fertilizer for growing anything out west.)

But let's wait to hear from the Swedes before we jump to any conclusions.

Some people claim that 35% of British Columbians want to leave Canada.

I live in B.C. for nearly 20 years and I'm sure that 35% of the people there don't know they live in Canada and have never been there.

They don't see Canada when they go on vacation either.

How can you leave some place you don't live and never visit?

And then there's Pete Laughe'ed. I was born in his great province of Alberta. That province is full of generous people who don't always express themselves very clearly.

A few years ago, as a for instance, some Albertans decide to tell eastern Canadians exactly how much they're needed to help the Alberta winter tourist industry.

So bumper stickers are printed up inviting easterners, including those who don't know their biological fathers, to share the experience of cold Alberta winter nights.

But, for some reason, the catchy slogan, "Let those eastern bastards freeze in the dark" just doesn't appeal to potential tourists.

Forty years later Alberta tries sweat talk again, spewing out pipe lines in all directions. The highest people in B.C. rejects this as a pipe dream.

At one point in the past, probably the most appealing news from the west, in recent times, is that the movie stars are finally ending their long strike.

So we'll finally be able to see all those TV shows that would have already been cancelled if they had begun in September, as usual.

In other cultural highlights out west – When the last word in fads is urban cowboys here in Toronto, out west everything is becoming a rural city-slicker.

Ranchers in the foothills ride to the range wearing uncomfortable business suits while reading carefully folded city newspapers.

When they get to the range, they hastily dismount, bump into each other, and elbow their way through a crowd of feeding cattle.

Then they spend the whole morning sitting around in swivel chairs, drinking Mr. Coffee coffee, and telling each other about what they saw on TV last night.

Out west sure ain't where it used to be.

Without direction

The Pacific Northwest is Siberia.

In Toronto, "northern Ontario" is Barrie and "out west" is just east of Kenora.

"The Northwest Passage" is an excerpt.

"Due South" is an invoice for cross-border shopping.

"Down east" and "down north" are in the same vicinity.

"The west coast" includes Stepenville.

"The coast" is for skate boarders.

Outports are out of vogue, many kilometres.

Inports are boats and ships during storms.

Delusion means shedding an illusion.

I've got you under my skin. So I'm going to see a dermatologist.

Headlines are wrinkles caused by reading small print news without glasses and worrying about the stories.

People from the U.K. cut their lips by using lip glass.

It's impossible to save a vegetarian's bacon.

When the U.S. NBC television programme, The Tonight Show is made in "beautiful downtown Burbank" California and starts each show with "Heerre's Johnny!" I joke:

The California Highways and Health Departments now consider The Tonight Show to be Carsonogenic.

What's the difference between Calgary and yoghurt? Yoghurt has culture. (an Edmonton joke)

Did you hear about the watch factory that uses second-hand parts?

Did you hear about the plumber whose reputation went down the drain?

The elevator business has its ups and downs.

I'm running into people waiting for elevators who paw at the ashtray between the door ports and then ask me where the cups come out of this "drinking fountain".

It makes me want to go out and buy a solar-powered sun lamp.

The solar system is out of this world.

The solar energy conference features panel discussions.

The petroleum business is the internal combustion engine of the economy. It's stocks are burning down the market and fueling climate change.

It's products are going down in history as fossil fuels.

Petroleum companies grease wheels to prevent friction from reducing sales and pollution.

My circuit at a gym includes exotic things called "bench press", "standing bicep curls", "upward rowing", "military press", "seated rowing", "hamstrung curls", and "universal leg press"

The combinations of puns and misinterpretations seem marvellous.

Having a couple of years in partisan politics, studies in journalism, experience in community journalism, and other writing for publication, I think I already know the press.

But I'm wrong.

I also think curls are only on my head. I know they can stick out and be knotted. What about downward rowing, toward the ocean?

I wonder if my gardening dad ever orders seed money. It can be useful in growing chicanery.

Passive prevention

Bruce is a diligent, hard-working person who makes sure that he delivers the work he promises. He keeps going right up to Christmas to get the job done.

When I mention that others don't reply to requests for estimates, don't show up, and lose interest, Bruce says, "That's the way things are around here."

A bigger contractor does some work for us. The last job they do involves about 30 days of work. It takes them four months do complete the 30 days.

Finally the Covid-19 pandemic arrives. This province does the best in Canada, perhaps in the world at stopping the virus.

Few people get the virus, there are few deaths and almost everyone recovers. So this province becomes a model for Canada.

Sure, staying home and doing nothing is an art here.

Hangoo humour is going radioactive? Aboard a KAL flight I see a documentary film describing a certain plant as "Korean" cabbage. It looks the same as non-Korean.

Years later, Hangoo's food nationaism involves Olympic games in Tokyo. According to Al Jazeera, Hangoo officials are testing all food served to their team.

Why? To make sure that none of it comes from Fukushima, site of an earthquake and tsunami that caused a nuclear plant to leak out radiation ten years earlier.

It never occurs to me to be wary of eating in Hiroshima or Nagasaki.

I first arrive in Hiroshima about 25 years after the U.S. becomes the first and only country to use nuclear weapons.

Today, unable to resist the opportunity to mock the Hangoo Olympic officials' food nationalism, I write a letter to the Korean Times newspaper:

"Al Jazeera news says South Korea's Olympic team is fed only meals tested against radiation from Fukushima's tragedy 10 years ago.

Meals for teams from "developed" countries are not.

So are South Korean athletes genetically vulnerable due to China's open air nuclear tests 60 years ago? That damaged DNA in South Korean athletes' ancestors?"

What does Robin say when he hears that Batman is engaged? -- Holy Matrimony!

Does diplomatic immunity enable a person to tolerate and bankroll people who spend their lives in cocktail parties, spy games, and ignore the repercussions of their squabbles for the ordinary people who end up dying or maimed in the wars that diplomats use to solve the elites' disputes?

Diplomatic immunity does nothing to improve sick societies or to prevent death.

Double over time means cramps.

A tap dance is a leaky faucet.

The pollination is also called a bee hive.

A cheap cruise is a financial bruise.

Only seafarers can sail through exams.

Some people in the U.S. must be students of Jacques Cartier. Thus they call the country north of them "Cainada".

A former Canadian ambassador to France, federal cabinet minister, and Québec premier says, "Canada is not a real country."

Faithful to his own words, while campaigning in support of a separatist referendum, he reassures wavering voters that that an independent nation called Québec will continue to use Canadian money and Canadian passports.

Unreal.

Twenty-six years later, a former cabinet minister in a former Québec separatist government returns to Canada after living in the U.K. for a number of years, vowing to found a new separatist party in Québec.

She was in the U.K. to study English and Scottish sepa-ratists or to preserve the French language by speaking English?

She says that her new separatist party will emphasize the environment and that forming a new nation-state called Québec is the surest way to solve all the problems.

Since the environment is a world phenomenon requiring global cooperation, how does creating yet another nation-state putting its sovereignty ahead of others' help the world in any way?

Take the nationalistic divisive nation-states system's abysmal record of trying to fight COVID-19. Please!

L.Q.

In the context of signs used by U.S. instigated and funded political agitators in Canada against the prime minister and Québec premier, the meaning of letters becomes apparent.

F.L.Q. is a vulgar insult to Le Québec.

Convictions

Convictions. Convicted. Convict. - Such are shortened terms of a long term.

Discovery

There's something much more exciting, stimulating, interesting, and fun than virtual reality.

What is this marvel?

Reality!

Uncommon language

The Japanese language is called Nihongo. English is Eigo. Chinese is Chugokugo. Every language is on the go, even if nobody knows where.

So what language do people living in the Shika area of Sawara-ku in Fukuoka speak? Shikago?

Forgotten words redefined

A rumble seat can be fore or aft. The name of this seat is also evidence of seismic activity or minor combat.

A running board is a disinterested marathoner.

A decal is an unmelodious musical.

Switchboard is a game changer or a replacement for a warped one.

Ann Alog doesn't hesitate but Digit Al freezes.

Communication is moving a phone.

On the line means a sucker hooked into buying a new phone every six months.

Cheapskates are on sale.

Both hands off deck

Somehow people can be shorthanded but not longhanded. Yet they can write both ways.

Having words

Order is demand or request. So disorder is cancel? A meeting is an appointment. The outcome of cancellation is disappointment?

I know mango. So does woman. A mangrove makes me wonder what's grove. A place where a man is planted?

Sophistication

Of all the subtle and widely misunderstood insults, the word sophisticated is near the top of the list. I would never want to be attached to that label.

Sophists were people who wasted much of their lives trying to determine how many angels could fit on the head of a pin.

Rebranding preoccupations

In my early teens I laugh when I hear that a building janitor friend of my parents starts calling himself a sanitary engineer.

But such rebranding seems commonplace today.

So many news interviews show titles under commentators' names declaring them consultants, analysts, and experts of this and that.

The unintended humourous results of the mass titling are only encourage me to expand this new trend by titling everyone I can imagine.

My rationale is that certain activities and behaviours seem to need further explanation or complete rebranding to describe them.

Syndicated features can be criminal activities or religionists' misdeeds.

A polite applied scientist is a civil engineer.

An athletic applied scientist is a physical engineer.

An intoxicated applied scientist is a chemical engineer.

A combined major in applied engineering and medicine becomes a truly sanitary engineer.

Martial arts are arresting, charging, and booking.

Members of "social media platforms" can be called exhibitionists, voyeurs, eavesdroppers, and gossipers.

The same words could be applied to hackers by adding thieves to the list.

"Gamers" can revert to their old designations: recluse and hermits.

Academics seem to be best described as pinheads, like their sophisticated predecessors. Or are they a mutation of a pandemic?

People running bank insecurity systems are definitely pinheads.

Gourmets and food tasters can be rebranded gluttons and moochers.

A panhandler should henceforth be called a fundraiser.

Any person who constantly tells her/his life story and talks about her family to complete strangers who just want to relax or enjoy the scenary during the ride on an intercity highway bus can be designated a communications expert.

A person who sits on a bench all day watching buses, trains, etc. going by can be labelled a transportation observer.

An advertising flyer delivery person is a special agent.

A job counsellor is an occupational therapist.

Personal ad: Seamstress seeking meteorologist in isobar.

More seriously, a grocery store worker on the job during a worldwide pandemic is an essential services provider in a high risk profession.

An African-American asked to pull over and stop his/her motor vehicle by a U.S. police officer becomes a crisis management consultant.

Disgruntled current and former employees are not management and organizational analysts. Some are weapons specialists, but only in the U.S.

Human trafficers are xeonerated by declaring themselves human resources exploitation specialists.

White collar crime experts can be called financial analysts and advisors.

Volume control designers and hard-of-hearing people can be redefined at audiological specialists.

Snake oil merchants can be rebranded medical and pharmaceutical supply providers.

Real estate agents are henceforth inflation enducement specialists and imagineers*. (*Overly loud hearing aids?)

Dentists will be called human resources exploration and exploitation experts.

A midwife is the second of three, five, seven, etc.?

Veterinarians treat the dogs of war?

A carpenter working as a private contractor is henceforth to be called a hammer and nail technician with clients.

A chimp in a saloon paying for the other primates' drinks is just monkeying around.

Lawyers can be categorized as weight scale consultants.

Parents will henceforth be more accurately described as psychologically troubled security guards.

People with all marital statuses will be called human relationship consultants.

All professors of religion will be defined as fundamentalists. So will anyone teaching beginners in any field of endeavour.

Other types of workers will have their titles simplified for broader comprehension.

Applications programmers become known as bureaucrats with forms.

Computer network professionals are keyboard typists, mouse wigglers, and screen tappers.

Database professionals are military statistics storage clerks.

Card players who drive while playing games are wheeler-dealers.

Software developers are silk worms.

A computer is a calculating person or a non-biological machine or tax collector.

Doctors and nurses are simply curators.

A dispatcher sending ambulances in response to emergency calls is now a medical communication expert.

Systems analysts are political scientists.

Performing artists are living ones with jobs.

Economists are yodellers in the mountains.

The can also be people on tight budgets who give creditors imaginative but fanciful excuses for non-payment of debts.

Translators and interpreters are gossip mongers.

A psychiatrist is an insecurity expert.

Shrinks in hot water are laundry consultants.

Flood victims are underwater explorers. So are mortgage speculators betting on defaults.

Formerly lowly couch potatoes who never venture beyond their routines, including docile, sedentary leisure, can now lay claim to an assortment of titles, making them much sought-after guests on interview broadcasts.

Couch potatoes can now be called analysts of all that they survey, on screen.

Their new designations include, but are not limited to, basketball analysts and political analysts.

They draw from years of sitting and watching people who have lives and actively participate in them.

Bored Japanese homemakers who live under a state of constant house arrest now become foreign exchange and rates strategists.

There is hope for sickly people or those who are chronically ill. The can now declare themselves infectious disease specialists.

During a story about unsafe disposal of toxic waste in Italia, Al Jazeera News describes a source on the topic as a "Mafia expert".

Does that mean someone in charge of organized crime, an employee of it, or a deceased victim of it?

It's so great that anyone can now have a title. How egalitarian!

But why limit the rebranding to people? Chairs and desks can now be labelled clerical support assistants.

A cane used by an office worker would be called office support staff.

A "kiss-and-tell" book would be a tattle tale. This might also be described as a legacy following the author.

Sick jokes

Boris Johnson, an architect of the U.K. separatist movement, is hospitalized, held in intensive care, and given oxygen due to the Corona Virus.

It's an ailment spreading out of control because the nation-states each try to go it alone instead of cooperating in a world-wide human health care movement.

Boris is later transferred to a different ward of the hospital. The psychiatric ward?

He holds a party not respecting any of the health measures that he imposes on the public. Unfortunately, it's not a lease on power breaking party. He only has to pay a fine.

Covid-19 goes viral everywhere, not just on the internet.

People needing medical care must be sickos.

A pandemic creates a sick society or highlights one that already is.

A witness before a government body solemnly swears that the antin-COVID-19 vaccine renders her magnetic.

Oh that it were true! It would finally enable us all to find that needle in the haystack.

The U.S. blames the COVID-19 pandemic on Chuang Hwa. It's a wonder that the chief U.S. pandemic advisor isn't accused of being Chinese. He is Dr. Fau Chi.

COVID-19 apparently adds to the sense of isolation already well established by the electronic devices atomization isolation of people.

The problems of santé mental don't translate as sentimental in English, but do they share the same semantic origins and results?

An operatic performance is surgery? It is in a theatre.

Versatile surgeons are equally competent at switchboards. They can be incisive and cut off callers.

My parents could become surgeons during my childhood because they have the knack of cutting me off television.

Good surgeons can work for the telephone company because they are smooth operators.

People who play card games must be sick. When they deal there's always something going around.

Some cutting situations do merit a bandaid solution. Melting a bandaid in hot water can have the same results.

Health workers must be good humourists. They keep patients in stitches.

Health workers have to be careful.

Books with too many extra sections at the end need an appendectomy.

A long flight can end after 24 hours flew.

A virus can be very influenzial on daily life.

A public speaker who falls ill can still be influenzial.

Vaccination is sinful. People needing one are in quite a state.

Sometimes good health is a shot in the arm.

Healthy people need outoculations?

Who's innoculation?

Innoculation has to do with the eyes?

Dr. Who prefers to remain anonymous.

Dr. Jeckyl protects his Hyde.

Dr. Death runs out of patience.

Secret operations can't be performed in theatres.

Doctors improve by practicing medicine. A doctor sets up a medical practice. Doctors create an entire time system for their practice. It's called doctors' hours.

Doctors don't stop practicing until they retire. So they never learn how to be doctors.

Doctors begin their carriers as prisoners of internment camps.

When a doctor's income is altered for tax purposes, an accountant becomes a health worker.

Unhealthy behaviour includes stealing from the mafia.
A good diet helps people in Nippon stay healthy.

Older people don't catch oldmonia.

Males often get hernias. It's a sex change?

Sore throats are angry.

Cyropractors can't help all pains in the neck.

Plastic surgeons repair bags for petroleum companies.

Only skunks don't suffer from a sprain.

Patients nurse wounds. Nurses serve baby drinks.

Giving birth to a nation must be excrucatingly painful.

Patients can avoid pain during surgery by taking anasthetic perspective.

Taking a pill isn't illegal. Nor is being one.

Governments can give voters more than one dose of bad medicine.

In Español there's no single dose.

Physiotherapists drink only carbonated beverages.

Placebo capsuls aren't spaceworthy.

Time capsuls have no medicinal value and can take long to digest.

Taking a powder can result in literally that.

Don't take prescription medications injest.

Prescriptions are filled out before use and emptied inside patients.

Pharmacists are government agricultural subsidies.

Cardiogrammes are beyond words.

A trauma ward can be the set for tragic drama.

Recovery occurs when a hospital blanket that falls off a bed is restored to its previous location.

Denture sellers clench deals.

Dentists drill holes in budgets.

Pharmacist tennis enthusiasts play chemistry sets.

Pharmaceutical companies don't produce formal wear.

Veterinarians who perform surgery on cats know that practice makes purrfect.

Veterinarians are not old Nazi soldiers.

After only one episode the new television series died. It crashed due to pilot error.

Consonant control
world of UEI

U, E, and I are the favourite consonants for beginning the sales pitches of techno merchants in the current era.

They lead us to mass Illiteracy, the Ultimate sick society Empire.

We sit at attention and follow the techno merchants' orders, not ours.

Together the consonants provide techno corps with UnEmployment Insurance for times to come, when a more thoughtful and demanding public requires and yearns for something much more substantial in life than the latest techno toys.

In that renaissance of natUral rEal Intelligence, people will no longer say, "I phone U Enough?" They will realize that the sole outcomes from patronizing techno merchants are:

Expect Unimportant Illusions instead of news and information.

UnImportant Excess Ultimately Eliminates Intelligence.

Unlimited Exposure causes Illness.

I see U are a tube from lack of Exercise. U2?

Instant contact Explains Unresponsiveness.

High speed wireless devices Undermine and Erode Intelligence more quickly.

UEI Disconnects

When will people finally realize obvious things:

How can a "wireless" device be plugged in and require a surge protector?

The first wireless is a radio. It has an operator.

Improved reception is ecstatic.

Techno corporate management will confess, "I Usually pad my Expense account."

Techno garbage will be redefined as Ugly Effluent I don't need?

I ran Elsewhere to Undo myself.

I am Undoubtedly the real Evil Empire, UnItEd stateless of the world.

Technocrats gnaw on people's brains.

Is there a tall circuit?

The arrival of digital television is music to sore ears for rabbits everywhere.

Computer view screens take Digit Alice.

The bus that hardly rolls
while my eyes do

One Thursday in the early part of the year, Goldbrick and I are sitting in the dining room of the adult education department minding our own respective businesses when the department head walks into the room, taps each of us on the shoulder and, in his verbose manner says:

"You, and you..., I want to see you in my office this afternoon."

Not long thereafter, Goldbrick goes upstairs to the head's den.

Later, after he's down a spell, I mosy upstairs to see if the head is going to expell me or ask how my motor skooter is running.

I walk into his den, ask if now is okay. He consents. I walk in quietly, sit in front of his desk, and stare at him.

He begins. "What are you doing this summer?" I reply that I hope to finish my Master's degree. "And then?" he quiries.

My answer is as indefinite as my plans. Then comes the pitch.

The head tells me there's a really interesting job going which involves travel in B.C. My eyes light up at the word travel.

He talks of collecting data for a Master's thesis or a Doctoral dissertation and establishing a reputation as an adult educator.

But he does say travel, and that's all I want to hear.

Besides, this is a celebrity offering, a noted adult educator and the head of my department, so who could argue?

If I weren't already thinking about enrolling in the Master's programme for more than a year, I could attribute that earlier decision to him too.

The day I make that decision I'm sitting in the adult education kitchen when the head plops down beside me and says, "Why aren't you in the Master's programme?"

The head always has trouble getting a straight answer out of me. This day is no exception.

My reply is that I've been wondering the same thing, I was enrolling.

He's pleased.

Back to the case in point, the day in his den. The friendly, unpredictable, ornary head is handing me a travel job so why argue.

Out comes the engraved, impressive-looking project brochure about its goal to take tape-recorded continuing education materials to various communities.

I virtually (almost) sign on the dotted line.

That's a good deal, I think, as I beam while striding out of the den. Salary doesn't come up. I'm tuned to the sound of adventure.

Goldbrick and I find out we're both to be nominated, as a team, to the head of the department running the project. No it's not our department's project.

The ten word title of the project is enough to impress us prairie boys. Goldbrick is from Manitoba and I'm from Alberta. The project title is: CEITHSMIRC.*

(*Seth's Mirc?)

The project is being funded by a Canadian government ministry, several foundations and professional associations, and a university.

We're to meet with the project head in a few days, so our head summons "You, and you." again, telling us to be careful what we say to the other head.

After all, we're the only people in our department with the essential qualifications: availability and enthusiasm.

The head of our department is absent the day of our meet with the other head which occurs in our department lounge.

Goldbrick and I don't meet the other head right away.

We spend the first hour of the meeting outside while a couple of our colleagues are selling the other head on the idea of hiring both of us instead of just one, and paying us equal wages.

We now hear that we could get more than $5,000 for 12 months work.

One of our colleagues tells us to act very enthusiastic about the project.

The project head isn't at all what I might be expecting. He's just a skinny, nervous little man with a slight English accent, not memorable at all.

When we finally meet, I'm amused by my expectations of a big man with a gruff voice and a lot of grey hair. Aren't all heads like our department head?

The project head says we can probably start on salary April 1, April Fool's Day, and be on the road by May.

He says he'll count on us to throw in a hand to help the students putting the finishing touches on the vehicle for this project, a 26 year old bus they are renovating.

I suggest, rather flippantly, that we'll count on the students to be finished by April 1. I guess the quip is too subtle for the project head.

He's the only one in the room who hardly even chuckles.

Later, as my days with the project go on, I will realize how hard it probably is for a serious person like the project head to keep his sense of humour.

At the "interview" he also explains that the bus has been worked on extensively by the students as a class project.

He proudly states that every part of the bus has been x-rayed by their school and remarkably little was found needing repair or replacement.

He also reveals that cooperation between his department and ours means we can get $6,000 for 12 months.

He says the rural centres we visit will probably feed us for free or at a very nominal rate.

The project head tells us to visit all the members of his project committee to assure their votes for our appointment as project field supervisors.

So the next afternoon we plan to make the visit to the project headquarters. It sounds like quite a task.

The morning of our visit I meet up with our department head while waiting for Goldbrick to show up. The head asks me about our meeting with the project head.

In answering I tell him about the afternoon's planned visits. His response can be summarized, in bluntness at least, as: "Forget it. No visits today."

An hour and a half later Goldbrick, a colleague, and I talk our head into reversing himself. So Goldbrick and I, I who is about to leave for the day, go to the project headquarters.

Everybody on the committee is very friendly and as soon as we walk into each committee member's office we're greeted with, "So, you're the fellows who will be driving the bus."

Driving the bus is a euphemism for "establishing a reputation as an adult educator"?

Our visits seem like anti-climaxes. One member reassures us that the project head could get us good wages because there's lots of money for the project.

But two committee members differ from their colleagues.

One is a person who was in Hawaii under the crimson sun. Another is Mr Hyde, who really seems not to be *with it* as far as the bus project is concerned.

He laughs a lot. As we relate to him what we're told about the bus, he puts his tongue in his cheek, showing us a photo of the shiny paint job on the bus.

It has a logo for a provincial centennial celebration held three years ago.

Pointing out this dated decoration he tells us not to expect any travel in that bus for the next four months, not next month.

While Goldbrick and I are leaving the project headquarters, I'm thinking that we have it made.

I'm chuckling too, wondering how that funny guy Hyde could be so out of touch with reality.

A few days later, our department head catches me streaking into the department kitchen in my orange scooter-riding suit, puts a friendly grip around my shoulder and says, "Your salary is $5,000."

I reply, "For the first six months?" "For the year," he retorts.

A mature student sitting next to him is disgusted and makes this clear to the head with some rather dismayed sounding comments about living costs being more than the salary.

The head defends himself by saying I'd be getting free sleeping quarters in the bus.

The salary is immaterial to me. A small net pay suits me fine.

But Goldbrick feels differently. Moments later he starts down the department staircase as the head ascends it.

When the head mentions the wages in passing, Goldbrick turns a little paler than usual and says, "That's a pity."

A later chat with Goldbrick and a colleague produces a memo to the head which helps give us the $6,000 Goldbrick wants.

As March comes to its third week, the head suggests that I join a department conference and study trip to Montréal during the last days of March and the first week of April.

I reply by asking if this would not interfere with my April 1 project job starting date. The head says there'll be no problem. So I go.

It's an all-expenses paid junket of sorts, with the airfare paid by the federal government and free accommodation at the Laurentian Hotel.

We're to visit some people working in adult education in Montréal and attend a conference with adult educators from other places too.

Before departing I tell Goldbrick that if the project people ask about me he can reply, "Oh Anderson - flew, he'll be away for a few days".

As it turns out, Goldbrick has to tell the project head that I have loose ends to tie up at our department, another quasi-truth.

The first project crisis strikes when I return from Montréal. Goldbrick later begins calling me the jinx, a distinction we are both to share.

The ruckus is over what colour the carpets and curtains will be in the bus.

But while a solution to that grave problem is being sorted out by the project commitee, Goldbrick and I work on a set of questionnaires to be filled out by each person entering the bus and using its facilities.

A reasearch assistant already makes a good start of the questionnaires, so all that Goldbrick and I really have to do is perfect them.

That's done in a round of meetings, some hours of which Goldbrick and I squander on giggling.

Some of my suggestions, I would rethink and tell Goldbrick that they leave egg on my face.

When I suggest that we ask bus users if they have physiological problems by asking if they wear contact lenses or hearing aids, Goldbrick brings tears of joy to our eyes by suggesting that a chicken has deposited something other than egg on my face.

A second task is largely done at my initiative. I think the project itinerary is bonkers. It seems to be written by someone totally unaware of the climate and geography of B.C.

We're given a free week which requires driving a long way. Some free week.

In early winter we're to be in part of the province noted for early snow. In early spring we're scheduled for notorious landslide areas.

I work on a totally revised timetable.

Then Goldbrick and I go over the old itinerary together and find that project locations are clustered soundly on the whole.

Goldbrick tells me that the project head is rigid on the itinerary and that he will object to even the changes called for by climate.

The project head already sends letters to locations enclosing the itinerary and asking if it would be a good idea to send the bus to their community.

I always think visitors should ask about coming at all before making a fixed travel plan, but then I'm just a field supervisor, not an administrator.

Anyway, the first set of letters are sent to the wrong places because secretaries receive lists showing the wrong places.

A second mailing has to be sent. A third mailing would probably make the project look even less well planned.

While I'm in Montréal, Goldbrick visits the bus and our department head tells me it's a long way from ready.

April is well underway and I'm getting anxious to do more to see that we get away by May. I'm gung ho to get the bus on the road, even if not until late May.

I push for trips to the bus to encourage earlier completion, and work to prepare the tape recorded materials and play-back equipment to install in the bus.

The carpet and drape colour controversy is swept away by a well-planned statement by Goldbrick at the first of our project committee meetings.

I'm prepared to report our progress with questionnaires at that meeting, but the committee runs out of time.

The committee gives Goldbrick and me our own office at project headquarters and a mountain of taped materials to sort out and order logically.

When April closes we find the missing committee member drifting back from the South Pacific. He tells us about how he buys the old bus for the project.

Originally, the project is to have a small trailer with facilities for one user at a time. But one day, this person and his children go for a drive.

His kids see the local transit company selling old buses at an auction. They tell their daddy to buy a bus. So he does.

Then he decides it should be the project vehicle. So off it goes for renovations by students at another educational centre. That' three years ago.

And there the bus stays, driverless until Goldbrick and I are hired.

Goldbrick and I are on the bus buyer's back for almost two months to get some of the bus materials from him. He begins to avoid us.

Apparently, his children are gettting paid for preparing the missing materials and he doesn't know where things are now.

One day a bright orange wrapped parcel with a matching ribbon mysteriously appears on one of our desks. It contains the missing materials.

When I find out who sends it I'm glad that he isn't sending us a bomb to do away with the bothersome field super-visors.

At some point, the same committee member who buys the bus gives us a copy of a letter that he receives from a United Nations body.

He portrays it as showing that the U.N. body is interested in the bus project.

Upon closer inspection, i.e. actually reading the letter, I find that it makes no mention of the project.

It is simply a covering letter for some information that the body is sending to the project bus buyer about training people in "developing" countries.

...

In the sorting tasks as in all other project tasks, Goldbrick has an uncanny ability to get stuck with the most tedious or complicated part compared. But I'm not.

Even when we flip a coin to divide up chores, which is most times, Goldbrick always gets the worst job.

Somehow, in one of our sorting tasks, I put a set of materials in alphabetical order in a rather unorthodox manner.

The set's last title begins with the letter "A". Goldbrick says not to mention it and nobody will notice. He's correct. We're not dealing with meticulous administrators.

Every time we go to Mr. Hyde for his division's contributions for the bus, he gives us a rather patronizing smile and tells us a story or two.

He says he wants to become a doctor in a big U.S. city hospital. He'll be Dr. Jeckle? He says he thinks he needs to go somewhere with lots of gunshot wounds to treat.

Talking about the project itinerary he mentions that his estranged wife lives in one of places on the list.

He says, in a vulgar way, that he thinks she needs one of us to sleep with her. He says not to tell him if we both do so.

It's not going to happen. We're not going to look her up when we're in town. But Goldbrick jokes about it when we get there.

Returning to our first weeks at the project office: Goldbrick and I are developing a master index for previously unsorted bus materials.

I think that a few copies of the index should be made and sent from the project headquarters to each location, just before the bus is supposed to arrive, along with advance public relations kits.

This package could be returned to the project office for remailing to other locations after our departure from the previous locations. Recycling.

This plan only involves sending indeces and public relations kits pre-packed for mailing back and forth.

The project head rejects the idea outright, just as Goldbrick predicts they will.

The head soon resigns from his two half days per week job as project head to get on with his regular job.

He remains interested in the project and returns many times to look at and criticize the way the project is run.

Many months later, in November, the project office starts sending indeces to locations.

Goldbrick and I have many visits to the bus where the students are supposed to be working on it.

The institution where they study is, I hope, the last vestige of the authoritarian post-secondary educational institution.

Their instructor's first name is "Mr." and he is the law who rules all.

You can't miss his office. The door displays his title, Mr., and his family name in nearly 30 cm font capital block dark bold letters.

Goldbrick and I have to make an appointment to meet the ruler in the building where the bus now sits.

We usually arrive two to fifteen minutes late on the cross-town expedition to get to that place. And if we see "Mr." at all, and sometimes we don't, it's three hours later.

One of the project technicians tells us that he spends an entire afternoon waiting for Godot, er "Mr.", with no results. So our experience is par.

Tyrants need not grant an audience to we mere disrespectful mortals?

The first time that I see the bus it's very dirty. I have no idea about the mechanical condition of the machine. That's the work of "Mr."s students.

But the two half days per week project head gives us a bright picture with his x-ray tale.

The bus interior is full of very impressive wood cabinet work.

This is the work of Jack L., the most efficient and one of the friendliest, most decent human beings involved in the bus project.

The electrical work, carpeting, and curtains seem to be the only delay keeping Goldbrick and me from taking the free bus driving classes that the two half days per week had arranges for us at the local transit company.

We run into a sort of Hyde-like character at "Mr."s school. He's in charge of the heavy mechanical work.

He says the bus probably has a life expectancy of more than two million kilometres and that it already goes more than half that distance during its years at the transit company.

He says we should pray a lot when operating the bus.

He says he works at "Mr"s school since the bus arrives there. He adds that, as far as he knows, there has never been an x-ray check of the bus.

Someone is lying to us?

By the end of June the bus is rolling away from "Mr."s school. The curtains are still not in.

Some "minor", unexpected problems arise. The air conditioning doesn't work.

That problem is straightened out by August by switching two wires connected the wrong way.

Another "minor" problem is that the reverse gear of the engine doesn't work. There is also no spare tire. There never is a spare tire during my time at the project.

Waiting time for bus parts also delays our departure.

Goldbrick is a changed man every time we go near that bus.

Around the office and our department he's full of laughs. He makes some funny mistakes, like me, and has a wonderfully outrageous sense of humour.

But that bus makes him tense, irritable, and sometimes downright cantankerous.

At first this inclines my eyes to pop out and my mouth to fall open. But I get used to it.

Eventually I find it so funny that I have to get a little ways from his eye and ear shot to burst out laughing without risking a punch in the shoulder.

He's that angry about the bus.

Goldbrick calls me raunchy, goofy, and some other things which I won't write.

He never can spell prince. He says, "Anderson, you're a prince", and then gives a real peculiar spelling of prince.

As time goes on he calls me Anderfottle and I dub him Goldbrick.

He has a rough time with his real name. Every time he introduces himself to someone s/he gets his name wrong. They call him Gobart or Boberg, or some other name.

Goldbrick has a booming, authoritarian-sounding, deep voice which causes him to be at the centre of any conversation.

At "Mr."'s school, this makes me feel almost invisible and sometimes a little uptight. But Goldbrick's pre-eminence just brings him insults from "Mr."

So I have no regrets about playing Goldbrick's straight man.

Sometimes I act as if Goldbrick is my office boy, just for laughs. When a delay in the project develops I tell him to "go tell those mugs to elevate their posteriors".

He responds by acting shocked.

I insist that we begin loading the bus to hasten our departure. So we do.

In May, Goldbrick and I are thinking about using data we collect in questionnaires for a Master's thesis each. This is what our department head leads us to believe is possible.

The temperature is 24-27°C in our hot* office. The air conditioning on our floor doesn't work either.

[*A typically warm summer temperature outdoors this month is about 20°C here.]

That's why our minds drift to bizarre schemes?

We start talking about taking the bus to Mexico. A full herd of secretaries in the project office say they want to be put on our waiting list for assistants in Mexico.

Before leaving the office, of course, we would write our theses and then spend time each week in Mexico filling out the questionnaires to substantiate our pre-written theses.

Some friends visiting me in June suggest that Goldbrick and I could have the necessary answers pre-printed with the questionnaires.

And we could hire people to scribble signatures on each questionnaire to make it look as if bus visitors in small towns had signed them.

But as time goes on, Goldbrick and I figure that the bus probably wouldn't be able to make it through the Sierras to get to Mexico.

[In retrospect, this idea is a bad one, but only because by taking a bus that doesn't work into Mexico we would only be contributing to the racist stereotype that buses always break down in Mexico.]

[Ultimately, there is no need for us to doctor our masters on a trip to Mexico. Soon after we arrive in one town the local weekly newspaper sends a reporter to interview us and he reports that we are "both holding a Masters in Adult Education".

This doesn't make the questionnaires and theses unnecessary, because the paper is literally saying that we're sharing half a degree each.

We both still have to work on the second degree following the reporter's third.]

Goldbrick starts to get sort of raunchy himself in June.

A September departure, he says, will suit him just fine. He tells me some hilarious stories about himself and his relatives.

Goldbrick's stories still make me just about roll on the floor.

We have to start closing our office door at the project centre so that the committee won't evict us.

People from our department drop in from time to time.

The head of our department comes in once with some big wig Yankee who asks us to describe the objectives of the bus project.

Goldbrick speels off an authoritative sounding reply in his authoritative sounding voice.

He later tells me that he thinks his answer is so inadequate that, "I feel like turning in my belly button."

Our department head hussles out the Yankee pretty fast.

Obviously, the objective of the bus project is to give Gold-brick and me holidays with pay, or so it seems to other graduate students at our department.

One not unkindly refers to us as a couple of con artists. Well, I don't know who is really being conned.

Instead of being on the road in May, Goldbrick and I suffer oxygen starvation and heat prostration in the concrete office building.

We can decide our own work hours and book in about 10:30 a.m. each day, "doctors' hours", and often drive hard to be done with the routine, sometimes boring material sorting tasks by 6 p.m.

But as we come to June and both Hyde and the project bus buyer come through with final materials, Goldbrick and I are getting a bit short on work.

The bus still isn't ready to roll.

Coffee breaks, juice to me, become rules instead of exceptions.

By mid-July, I'm drawn away from the office for full lunch hours, or hours and a half by the university summer student society noon concerts on the campus lawns.

Goldbrick and I are impressed by the effort that "Mr"s school puts out to finish the bus by their June end term closure.

By the middle of May, Goldbrick and I pick up our learners' licences at the motor vehicles branch. We receive our licenses as bus drivers before the middle of July.

The bus is pushed or driven out of "Mr"s school in the later half of June by our local public transit bus drivers' driving teacher. He's Johnny.

Johnny turns out to be one of the most cheerful and patient talents we come across in the bus project.

It takes about three weeks of bus breakdowns before Johnny starts to feel sort of discouraged about the whole bus project business.

His first problem comes the day he picks up the bus from the school. The bus fails the standard provincial government safety inspection test for motor vehicles.

During the weeks that follow, while learning to be bus drivers, Goldbrick and I spend a number of mornings in air brake classes, again free to us through the public transit company.

In the afternoons we try to learn bus driving through practice rides with Johnny.

After two more attempts and several visits to the transit company garage, the bus finally passes the safety inspection test.

The first garage visit is for a carburettor adjustment. The transit company's head mechanic does the job in a few minutes, using a screw driver.

He refers to the project bus as "an old pig", a term which Goldbrick already uses to christen the tired old wreck. I call it "the monstrosity".

But we label it with another word. The front of the bus includes the original destinations on a rolling display sign. Goldbrick and I agree on the one saying "Special".

A better ironic display would be "Out of Service".

A few visits to the garage later, the head mechanic says that the bus is so bad that he wouldn't go beyond the city's region in it, even with his own tool box.

The head mechanic is the public transit system's most proficient and experienced bus mechanic.

As we drive the project bus into the garage for the second time, one mechanic says to me:

"Why would the university throw away money on an old hunk o' junk like that?! They've got plenty of money. They should buy something decent."

One of the best test rides we have is to a pleasant waterside resort called Deep Cove. Goldbrick is driving. He follows the road that parallels the cove side.

There's no sign indicating a dead end so we're surprised to find the narrow road ending abruptly. Goldbrick has to back along the twisting street for a good kilometre.

I stand out in the middle of the road waving him back.

Our test rides are constantly disrupted by overheating of the bus engine.

We spend a lot of driving time sitting under trees and in air conditioned hamburger joints waiting for the bus engine to cool off.

But when the clutch slipping problem begins, we rush back to the transit company garage at 50 km/hr. Once we don't make it. We're marooned in New Westminster.

Our confidence in the project bus undergoes substantial declines.

After less than half the training that a regular public transit bus driver receives, Goldbrick and I are fully licensed.

As July moves into its second half I suggest that we go on a test ride to Squamish.

By a coin flip Goldbrick ends up driving from Vancouver and I'm to drive back. It's just another case of Goldbrick losing a flip as it turns out.

We make it as far as Horseshoe Bay going a moderate speed downhill and less than 30 km/hr going uphill.

But beyond the Bay the project bus is finding half that speed a strain. Then it stops in the middle of the highway.

We're in first gear, going nowhere, poised on an upgrade, and smoking at the gearbox.

I think about putting out the emergency flares as the mad drivers of Squamish road wiz past.

Golbrick says, "Collision."

I hear brakes scream and the frightening crunch of glass and metal. I feel very uncomfortable. Visions of heads rolling down the highway make my heart sink.

We rush out, Goldbrick first. What a mess.

One car is parked on our backside, sandwiched in by another car jammed against the highway ledge's concrete sidewall.

Goldbrick is cool, steady, and keeps things rational.

The car occupants al get out of their vehicles with only minor cuts, scratches, and bruises.

How pitifully unnecessary this scene is, I'm thinking. I carefully scrutinize the accident scene.

I'm deeply touched by a woman around my age in the centre car who slowly walks to the most secluded side of our bus and bursts into tears.

She's in the last days of a visit from her home in Montréal. I'm peeved. An innocent bystander of the bus project is suffering.

A bus with the word "education" painted in 30 cm high letters is sitting in the middle of a highway surrounded by wreckage.

The bus project is drawing blood and tears.

This project is now too expensive for my taste.

A few police interviews for witnesses and two tow trucks later, the project bus is back at project headquarters.

Our stay on the roadside is prolonged when the driver of a regular sized tow truck decides that his vehicle doesn't have the strength to risk towing the project bus.

I sit by roadside trees contemplating my next move.

I'm already prepared to resign in July. The climate is ripe for it.

Other events cause a falling out between our department head and the project people.

Seven key members of the project staff leave since our arrival in April. And not because they don't like our jokes either.

I decide to do a Sam Irwin* on the project committee instead of just dropping them like a soggy tobacco plug.
[*A famous U.S. Senator exposing the Watergate Scandal at the time.]

Independent of Goldbrick and without his knowledge, I turn up at the post-accident special project bus committee meeting with a memo calling for a complete investigation of the old bus to assure that it's capable of fulfilling the project's demands.

I add that even the public transit company's chief mechanic says he won't go beyond the city's region in the project bus.

I know that a thorough study will force the project committee to use a better vehicle.

Reading my report, the committee chairperson says, "Of course we wouldn't send you out in a dangerous vehicle".

Had she only been on the Squamish road with the Montréal woman or in New Westminster when the clutch failed.

Yet the chairperson is fully aware of these events, though her colleagues on the committee apparently are not. The chairperson must have taken the hypocritic oath, I think.

When the chairperson comes to our office the next day, without the pose or poise of the meeting, and attempts to brow-beat me into an apology for not telling her about the memo in advance, I reply that I accept full responsibility for the memo.

I look right through her. From that day forth I am just in the project for the money. A September start would suit me fine.

The special meeting refers my memo to a further special meeting with the chairperson, the bus buyer, Goldbrick, the transit company chief mechanic, and myself.

At the second special meeting, the chief mechanic is a regular Little Lord Fauntelroy.

He says he envies Goldbrick and me. In fact he now claims he offered to pack his own tool kit and come along with the project bus for the ride.

He is no John Dean, at least in terms of his memory of past events.

He now says there are no guarantees, but that we would be all right to head well beyond the city's region in the bus.

When Paley said, "I have seldom known anyone who deserted truth in trifles, that could be trusted in matters of importance." he had not met the chief mechanic.

By revising and reversing his previous words, the chief mechanic effectively made our safety his responsibility.

My proposed investigation, which would have given the project a reasonable vehicle, would not occur.

So I will not be a part of the project after the last day of September.

I want no part of the desperate fanatacism which seems to be gripping the bus project committee chairperson. The defective bus would, it seems, run at any cost.

[I do not know the contents of the police report about the accident on Squamish road. I doubt that my memo is part of the insurance company records of the accident. I only know that Nixon resigned in disgrace the next year.]

The day that the chairperson comes to chastise me she also attacks Goldbrick. Evidently he makes a sarcastic comment to the project bus buyer. Goldbrick says he said:

"You could use a few lessons on how to buy a bus."

I almost burst with laughter at the chairperson's virgin aunt recounting of the tale of Goldbrick's terribly honest words to the bus buyer.

But Goldbrick, always ready to patronize appearances, tells me after the chairperson leaves our office that he had been stupid to say what he said to the bus buyer.

Goldbrick later goes to the bus buyer and apologizes.

I never understand why the bus buyer sends the chairperson to our office to express his offence to us for Goldbrick's appropriate and well-deserved criticism of the bus buyer.

All delegated powers of the members of the department are recalled by the chairperson. Everything becomes centralized under her thumb.

One day I casually mention a bus project problem to a member of the division and the chairperson reprimands him for the conversation.

His resignation soon follows.

The crumbling of an incompetent power structure, something I read about in political science books, is occuring now before my eyes.

It's probably only the departure of Goldbrick and me during the last week of July and the chairperson taking a year-long sabbatical that keep the department boyant.

The bus buyer becomes the new chairperson of the project.

By the time that Goldbrick and I leave in the bus, Goldbrick is very concerned about the future of the project.

He's counting on the money and he still has a slight hope of getting a thesis out of the project.

Meanwhile, I'm spending the hours of 8 a.m. to 10 a.m. on campus each morning figuring out a project to complete my Master's degree.

I'm toying with the idea of federal government official language training as a subject area, but there isn't enough time between deciding against a study based on the bus project and leaving town in the bus.

Goldbrick and I set out on a test week in a nearby town at the end of July.

We are scheduled to be on location the day before and the chairperson departing on sabbatical is quite upset that we are not.

But we have trouble with the old bus the Friday before and it remains in the garage the day we are supposed to be at the test week location.

That Friday, Goldbrick and I go to Squamish with a new clutch. This time we go all the way there without incident.

I drive there. We stop in front of a park for an open air lunch. We park in the street between two electric poles about two bus lengths apart.

After lunch it's Goldbrick's turn to drive, for the return trip back to the office.

But the reverse gear, which works perfectly when I maneouvre the bus to park it, no longer functions.

Goldbrick is angry with the bus. His anger obliges me to go to a neutral corner and choke down the giggles that his anger over the bizarre situation causes.

So long as Goldbrick can get angry, I can have something funny to give me the jollies.

It's not his anger that makes me laugh, just the cause of it.

Comedy and pathos do have their overlaps.

So why does Goldbrick apologize to the bus buyer and why does the chairperson departing on sabbatical deny reality and get angry when it bites her?

Someone from a local garage helps Goldbrick and me get around the telephone poles. We drive right back to town and the transit company garage before it closes.

After the mechanic fixes the reverse gear on Monday, we leave for the nearby town.

We arrive there without breakdown.

So here we are in a place that is expecting us to arrive almost every week in July.

The project bus doesn't have any curtains yet. So we place aluminum foil on the windows to keep the street lights out at night and the sunlight out at 6 a.m.

Nobody is feeding us. In fact, we have to wink and blink to get access to a cafeteria that is, according to the former project head, supposed to give us meals.

After all, the town hotel has good food, just down the road, or so we're told.

When we are granted entry to the cafeteria, the meals are neither nominal nor free as the person hiring us leads us to believe.

Wired power at the local project parking site makes the audio-visual equipment and air conditioning work.

But once on the road, beyond Hope, much beyond, we find that the bus generator isn't powerful enough to run the air conditioner.

(The generator is replaced by a larger one late the following year, I'm told.)

Supplement:

Although we find many friendly hospitable people along the road, there are occasions when administrators give the impression they consider us more a nuissance than bearers of a potentially valuable educational service.

Meals are rarely free.

The bus makes frequent stops for overheating, but makes it through Rogers Pass, going west.

It has to be towed from near Canyon Hot Springs to Revelstoke. It's later towed part way from Salmon Arm to Merritt.

At the end of August I submit a month's notice of my intention not to renew my contract for a second six months. Fortunately, it's not a 12 month contract.

In September the bus buyer resigns from the project committee.

Goldbrick is interviewed by radio and television. He gives the impression that everything is rosey and no problems ever occur.

I decline an invitation to give the same interview in French.

Two years later, in the early part of the year, I speak with a communications person working at the project office. He says Goldbrick is still with the bus project.

The communications person says the equipment is all removed from the old bus and it had been a mistake to use the old bus. My memo is finally heeded?

I feel sorry for Goldbrick.

The final joke is on him and the taxpayers and donors supporting the bus project.

Canada Rocks

Why are the Canadian Rockies always stoned? They go through long periods of upheaval.

The Canadian Rockies must be bad card players. They have a long history of folding.

Frank Slide is not a place to toboggan. Hope Slide is hopeless.

Cuts in northern Ontario are too gapping for bandaids and stitches.

There are so many falls in Canada that it's a wonder anyone can walk.

Canada has large islands on all three of its coasts, but few can see the enormous size of the country in between.

The Grand Banks of Newfoundland are insoluable or insolvent. Are they on the edge of an outport named Poggy, or is it Pogey?

"Moracho"

Alicia and Antonio have us over for an asado dinner after taking us on our first car tour of Buenos Aires. We always walk and take public transit.

The following day they're inviting us to lunch in a restaurant. At some point the table server learns that I'm from Canada.

At this point he says that the Canadian ambassador eats there, and he's "moracho".

The word is new to me in Español, so I reply "Is that good or bad?"

He replies that Argentinos are not racists.

Several tables of people are laughing as I try to make clear that I don't know that "moracho" is a dark skin tone.

"Dirty" story

Despite all the problems I have with some obnoxious gringos working at one particular L.B.E., there is at least one story giving this time a moment of comic relief.

To avoid going bonkers using the L.B.E.'s picture book and word list book, and to try to introduce some reality into the "method", I become creative and imaginative.

The picture book includes a drawing of a man shaving while a woman is taking a shower in the opaque shower stall behind him.

Part of the "method" requires students to describe the scene through a standard, widely-used question-and-answer teaching technique that the L.B.E. claims is unique to it.

The general description of the shaving and showering is always going to say that the man is shaving while his wife is taking a shower. All the students are adults.

In my mischeviously creative version of the story, when an adult student says the wife is in the shower, I shake my head and say the woman showering is the man's secretary.

The meaning of this situation is debatable, but students always find my version of the picture amusing and laugh. It livens up the "method", if only for one lesson.

My mischief does not amuse the next teacher, who has to review what I just complete teaching.

After his lesson he comes storming out of the classroom, extremely angry with me.

By this time, my previous class isn't foremost in my mind, so I'm wondering what he's talking about when he lashes out at me for "teaching filth".

My verbal assailant is chronologically younger than I am and he's a churchist missionary posing as a teacher for visa purposes. So his superior morality is pretence and dubious.

When I figure out the cause of his rage I can only break into a puzzled smile.

Another teacher, overhearing the one-sided conflict, attacks the missionary. She can't believe he's getting so hostile about what she considers to be nothing.

My harmless prank thus unintentionally creates more mirth than I expect and gives me some unexpected extra laughs.

"Editor" & "wife"

I almost become a name in the news, without doing anything newsworthy, due to a misunderstanding involving a current affairs issue.

At the time, there's a debate in Nippon, led by locals of Hangoo origin who are somehow considered non-locals after generations of residency here.

They have to carry "alien registration cards" like the temporary residents staying for more than three months.

Although the locals of Hangoo origin apparently don't mind being considered non-locals, they do object to having their fingerprints on the cards, as if they were booked in a police station for committing a crime.

I understand their point. I'm never fingerprinted, even when the military dictators rule Brasil, Argentina, and Chile.

For my Carioca friend Zita, fingerprints on identification cards are a norm for Brasileiro(a)s in Brasil going back to at least her eighteenth birthday, four years after the coup d.état overthrowing democracy in Brasilia.

I don't take part in the public debate about fingerprinting non-locals in Nippon. I already have my identification card bearing my fingerprint. I don't resist during fingerprinting.

But the editor of a local newspaper phones me at my work-place one day to ask me how it feels to be the first "U.S. citizen "to refuse" to be fingerprinted".

Here, finally, is a rumour that I don't start about myself.

I brush aside the insult that I have the right to vote and influence policy decisions in the U.S. Talk about not getting basic facts correctly- and this is an "editor".

I tell the "editor" I'm just a Canadian, not a representative of the good or bad deeds of the U.S.

Then I ask him to tell me the source of the false story that I'm refusing to do something.

He says that some churchist person hears the story from "my wife".

I ask the "editor" what language the churchist and my "wife" are using to communicate.

I add that the woman in question is a lusophone who doesn't dominate either English or Japanese.

Therefore, if the churchist doesn't speak Portuguese, I wouldn't put much confidence in anyhing that the churchist quotes from the person s/he calls my "wife".

I also don't recall marrying anyone. Who is "my wife"?

The editor apologizes and hangs up.

News speak

When nitpicking editors rule the news business, they are merciless to reporters who make mistakes, particularly factual mistakes. Spelling and grammatical errors are intolerable.

However, the Newseum in Washington, D.C. plasters some of its walls with news quotes that somehow make it to the eyes and ears of the news consuming public.

They're hilarious and rightly adorn the toilets of the building.

I find one such goof in a BNN Blumberg news headline. It says:

> China Warns Canada
> Goose May Have
> Broken Consumer Law

So Canada is held responsible for all the fowl things that go on in Chuang Hwa?

The headline may be an exceptional incident at the business-oriented news company. But maybe not.

Unfortunately, anglophone and anglophile news editors and readers at the equally professional N.H.K. News and a private broadcaster in Nippon, at least in the English language newsroom, provide an all too consistent diet of bloopers.

It makes me wonder if they care about making the news sound silly.

The anglohones at NHK, with some exceptions such as former CBC News journalist, the late Lorne Saxberg, seem to confine their interest in English language news to saying some things without noticing what they're saying.

If anglophones mangle their mother tongue, so much for making English "the world language". English is already mutating as if it were Latin. Heard of Singlish?

Journalism is full of expressions to help journalists do better jobs. If the one of thinking of is not already on the list, please add it:

Bad language usage is bad news.

Misspoken news

I'm always enjoying playing with words. I like to change their meanings and create unconventional vocabulary.

In this way I can distinguish one thing from another by using new ways of describing some activity, event, etc.

I also challenge word usage that isn't based in reality and make up ridiculous puns.

I'm setting out to do all of the above. It's part of my character and style. I'm using words to provoke thought and to improve language.

But here in Nippon, I'm hearing other people, anglophones, who must be naturals at word play.

Unfortunately, they're doing it without trying, without any effort at all, and for no apparent positive purpose.

Of all the incompetent or confidence artists working the English language scam in Nippon, the anglophone news script readers on bilingual sound track TV, on at least two different channels, are leaving all the rest behind.

They're at the top or bottom of the pile, depending on your perspective.

The simple reading errors of the anglophones I'm hearing are so blatant that these script readers are either not capable of speaking their own first language or deliberately and cynically taking money for reading writing they must know is full of very obvious and easily corrected errors in English.

Maybe they have little experience with and knowledge of their first language, like so many make-believe "English teachers".

Maybe they rarely watch and pay very little attention to the professional anglophone newsreaders in their homelands.

The anglophone news readers don't seem to care what's in their scripts. They're definitely not showing any evidence of being authentic, well-trained news broadcasters.

Only their voices and manner of delivery sound polished, not what they read.

Real news readers are taught to carefully read the news stories in advance and to correct errors instead of broadcasting them.

As usual, I'm listening carefully and taking detailed notes that justify my comments.

My tuning in doesn't start that way. I merely want to listen to news but end up not liking what I'm hearing.

Here are just a few examples of what news readers are unintentionally(?) telling me in only a few consecutive days of television news broadcasts:

A murder story becomes magical when the anglophone reader says that a killer "turned himself into a police box". It'a disguise to escape being arrested!?

One of the oldest chicken jokes in the world comes to mind when one anglophone script reader says, in a monotonous tone, with no hint of a chuckle, someone was "crossing the street to go to the other side".

Or is this just an exercise in being long-winded?

The anglophone script readers seem to be going far beyond unintended humour.

They're apparently intent on changing not just the English language but also the entire world that it describes.

All the world's problems must have been solved. Not really, but the anglophone news readers say people are "solving issues", instead of problems.

How do you solve an issue? Stop talking about it?

Apparently something is "generating" concern. Does that mean causing? So why not just say so?

At the same time, every problem is now becoming a trouble, such as "computer troubles". This is taking simple engine trouble and trouble-shooting too far.

Try to figure out this phrase: something "caused troubles with the customers".

The next question arising in my mind is this: Why is every type of public gathering now called a "rally"?

Even when the event is not a rally at all, but only a calm, restrained, docile meeting of people sitting sedately in the padded chairs of an auditorium, this is called a "rally".

Rallies that I see in times past consist of people standing in large, sweaty crowds either cheering and applauding spontaneously and enthusiastically, or following the lead of some kind of cheer leader.

In the mouths of the anglophone script readers, grammar is also harmed beyond recognition. Grammar becomes more than incorrect. It becomes a matter of random usage.

In one story, the electors "voted tremendously against" someone or something. How do they do that? Is "tremendously" on the ballot?

In another story, "a bear seriously inflicted a wound". To my knowledge, a bear is not usually reflecting upon her/himself before, after, or while inflicting wounds.

Bears do not humorously inflict wounds.

Measurement becomes totally unclear. An object is described as "two centimeters in size". Objects now have only one dimension? But which one?

Political systems are completely altered with the turn of a word.

Apparently, it has been a month since the latest cabinet in Tokyo is "incorporated". During the next repetition of this news story, the cabinet is "inaugurated".

Why not use the simple description- "sworn in" or "takes office"?

Government offices are being transformed every time that the script readers open their mouths.

After decades of deputy-prime ministers in Canada and elsewhere, the script readers unilaterally transform them all into "vice-prime ministers".

I know that in theory parliaments choose a prime minister, but a deputy-prime minister is simply a cabinet post filled by a prime minister alone. Parliament does not vote on it.

Nobody elects a deputy-prime minister. To my knowledge, this position is not in Canada's constitution or traditions.

The party in power, the group that news broadcasters in Canada simply and routinely call "the government", is being called "the ruling party" by some anglophone news readers abroad.

It sounds autocratic and dictatorial. It doesn't sound like an elected body.

If the news is about the party in power in Nippon, then why not just say "the LDP-Komei coalition government".

When only referring to the party with the most seats why not call it "the LDP government"?

At the same time, everyone working for the government is

called an official. It's a word I associate with football referees and other sports judges or adjudicators.

Instead of saying the police, a government spokesperson, a ministry source, the city clerk's office, etc., all these people are lumped together and given the shorthand title "officials".

Listeners are supposed to guess what kind of "officials"?

Anglophone script readers also seem to be having trouble distinguishing between government offices and corporate executive offices.

Sure, companies do seem to rule over or at least manipulate nation-state governments. But that's unofficial and behind the scenes, rarely direct, overt, and open.

Yet one anglophone script reader is calling someone a "company official" instead of a company director, executive, manager, spokesperson, etc.

Officials who are official are usually government people in certain special jobs. Companies don't have officials.

People in less ostentatious positions are getting changes in their job titles too. The anglophone reader calls one person a "half-time janitor".

Or does this means someone who only works as a janitor during the half-time shows at professional football games?

Physical objects too are getting renamed by the script readers. The camera shows a fence and the script reader says it's a "hedge". Glasses needed?

Human progress is getting erased too, by reviving discarded, inaccurate, and archaic vocabulary.

Thoughtlessly turning back the clock to the bad old days of rampant, overt sexual discrimination, one anglophone script reader with a U.S. accent calls police officers "policemen".

There are no more females in the police forces?

Always a marginal area of English usage, sports vocabulary is being sent into a remote exile. Forget about conventions in sportscast word usage.

The sports report is introduced as the sports "section". The TV folds into a newspaper?

A few years after the most recent olympic games held in Nippon, the pronunciation of Nagano is suddenly changed to Naaa gano.

An anglophone sports report script reader goes through a lengthy, roundabout way of describing professional sports players becoming "free agents" instead of being completely at the mercy of team owners.

But the reader never says "free agent".

There are no more semi-finals, finals, championships, series, or competitions.

Every sporting event, except the U.S. baseball "world" series, now becomes a tournament. I thought that word was for golf.

In other entertainment news…

A music competition is described as "one of the most established", which means exactly what?

Another competition must then be "least established"?

I thought such events could be more established, not most.

Or are we trying to say best known, oldest, most famous, most prestigious, etc.?

The education system is changing altogether. Students in grade eleven are now transformed into "second year high school students".

So the readers agree with me that elementary school grades are a forgettable waste of time and can thus be ignored?.

The word pupils has disappeared. Now six year olds are called "students", even by Canada's most trusted news script reader.

One report says a student is "tripped up", not tripped, by classmates. I get tripped up by words, but never by people. Besides, when I trip, I fall down, not up.

Consumer product labels become incomprehensible.

The very clear words "expiry date", as printed on processed, packaged foodstuff, are now described as the "eat-by-date" by an anglophone script reader.

So, to generalize this blanket usage of "eat-by", it means that people are now eating drinks, household chemicals, and medical supplies?

Now for the weather report –

During a story about a tornado, the script reader keeps re-peating the word "vortex", but never says "funnel cloud" while supposedly describing in English the first-hand ac-counts of people who see the tornado funnel cloud.

The anglophone readers go on to say that thunder clouds "generated" the tornado.

What's wrong with using a straightforward, quickly under-stood word such as "started", "stimulated", "caused", etc?

A "weather official" is then quoted. Does this mean a me-teorologist or a forecaster? Is the weather an official en-tity? Does the weather appoint a spokesperson?

It's hard to imagine a weather report rendered incompre-hensible, but the anglophone script readers strike again in the farthest reaches of Nippon.

Apparently, a house in Hokkaido is using "sheets" to pre-vent rain from leaking through rooves there.

This image of bed linen is contradicted by a TV camera showing plastic tarp.

"Body warmers" are being delivered to homes without heat. Could this mean a special type of rescue team or very large hand warmers?

Reporting from the courtroom –

Somebody is "charged with window-dressing" by the po-lice. I wonder what section of the criminal code describes the crime of "window-dressing".

People who decorate display windows in department stores

are now criminals?

Employers hiring certain individuals based entirely on their ethnicity, skin pigmentation, or sex, etc., for the sole purpose of avoiding accusations of racism and sexism, are now getting charged with breaking the "window-dressing" law?

Instead of saying that a witness or defendant will be testifying in court and cross-examined by lawyers, s/he is now attending a "questioning session".

Without any court case pending or criminal charges, an anglophone script reader says "allegedly the government". Is the government called "allegedly"? Or is it being charged?

How about describing a formal allegation and attributing a critical remark before turning to inappropriate, defensive legalese in the news?

Shorthand gibberish is reaching new lows too. France and the U.S. military are famous for mysterious acronyms and redefining words.

In that context of creating confusion and obscuring reality, what does this mean? –

"Over a week has passed since the advent of the cell phone portability system."

It means a general communications problem to me, regardless of the cell phone.

Weren't cell phones already portable? Isn't advent a bit literary or churchy for a simple newscast?

Well-trained broadcast journalists are instructed to say

"more than", unless describing something that is literally, physically "over" something else.

What's wrong with saying something clear and accurate, such as:

"It's only a week now, since the cell phone companies started making their products more compatible and inter-changeable..."

I know this is what the news is supposed to be reporting because Mariko translates a Japanese language version of the story.

In other news...

Something is "expected to start from next year". How about some economy of words? Why use both start and from together when a simple "start" is ample?

And finally:

On several occasions, one anglophone script reader is ending the regular, daily, 40 minute news programme by calling the entire broadcast a "bulletin".

There's no English-English dictionary in the television studio office?

When U.S. news host Walter Cronkite briefly interrupts regular television broadcasting to announce that JFK is shot dead, Cronkite says it's a "bulletin".

The militarization of all things is apparently another objective of the anglophone news readers. They use the word "decomission" for everything that moves or does not.

The only decommissioning that I know is about taking war ships out of service and scrapping them. The word decommission is related to the term "non-commissioned officer"?

Decommission is a word with specific military usage, not a universally applicable word for all things.

Restaurants and vaccinations are being jumbled together too, at least in terms of arranging encounters with them.

Now people are making "reservations" to get COVID-19 shots, instead of appointments. So we can all make an "appointment" to get on an airplane too?

How about making a "reservation" for a root canal?

Ill literacy

Unfortunately, anglophone and anglophile news readers far beyond Nippon are now almost routinely annoying me by misusing "an amount of people" to mean "a number of people".

They're not talking about a burial mound containing an uncountable and unassembleable number of body parts.

They are also tending to put the word "more" or "less" in front of words instead of adding -er or -est to make them bigger or smaller.

Why say "more good" when there is a better word?

In this news speak, "there is" always becomes there's and the plural, there are, is a forgotten set of words. There's only two words in there are?

News is breaking like wind?

Public B.S.?

I primarily critique N.H.K. anglophone news readers for their poor script writing, editing, preparation, and reading, but now I find the high quality U.S. P.B.S. Newshour is flawed too.

I hear "infuriorating" instead of infuriating; "He got less votes and less seats" instead of fewer; "it's becoming more and more clear" instead of clearer; "in two hours time from now"; and "go through much less doses".

It's not just N.H.K. and P.B.S.. Anglophone news is in trouble.

In other news I hear reporters saying "less people" instead of fewer or a smaller number of people, just like N.H.K..

A tremendous "amount" of people sounds like a huge archaeological site involving a mass burial mound full of body parts.

Weirder still are documentaries about people "wilding" the world. "Wilding" is not a real word.

They mean to say, in English, restoring the natural environment and natural species habitat and behaviours.

It's also simply and accurately called restoring nature or doing environmental reclammation work.

Why not explain what you're talking about instead of trying to reduce it to silly, nonexistent shorthand? People understand best when they hear clear language.

Unfortunately, the very reliable, accurate, and truly worldwide news service of Al Jazeera suffers from the same or similar English problems as the U.S. P.B.S.

Sometimes it is the bad influence of anglophones on the non-anglophone reporters. It probably also points out the great shortcomings of L.B.E. "language classes".

Problems can start with nation-state officials too. Former U.S. President Bill Clinton turns grow into a different type of verb.

Instead of helping the economy grow, Clinton insists on "growing the economy". You can grow carrots and raise livestock, but you can't "grow" an economy.

Clinton believes that seed money grows an economy?

Avian inalienation

A Canadian chicken meal seller advertizes that at his company they "parle poulet". Yet I never hear any offensive language.

No male sibblings

I ride in many assenceurs but I never find an assenfrère.

Guardian

Avant garde is a bumper against the anachronistic and reactionairies?

The Rule of Pedantocracy

To ensure our rule, we tell you what to do and you do it. That's how the system works, or doesn't. You have no say in it. Your elected representatives only imagine they do.

Our job is to invent forms which you must fill out; to casually read your answers on them; and to ask you more questions based on your answers in order to delay and deny service to you.

This is the origin of the term "provide public service". It means that you, the public, serve us.

Always fill in every item in the detail that we demand on the forms that we create and always meet our deadlines.

Your answers must never conceal, mislead, or lie. Otherwise you will be prosecuted for committing a criminal offence against pedantocracy.

If you refuse to answer our questions, you will be heavily fined and/or jailed by pedantocracy.

Only we can be unresponsive to your questions, evasive, corrupt, and dishonest, and ignore you altogether.

If you do not fill out the form completely and in the manner that we demand, you will be punished by us and we will do nothing for you.

If, however, you obediently submit everything that we want, completely and on time, you might eventually receive service, some day, even though we have no need to actually serve you and no intention of doing so.

Our best case scenario is that you give up, or better yet, die.

Don't get your hopes up. You won't live long enough to get service from us.

Regardless of the outcome, you must always pay us a fee in advance. Our motto is: No fee; no service. and, Pay fee; no service.

We may call the fee by various names, such as an administration fee (even though we receive full salaries for administration work and we don't get a bonus for serving more people more quickly and more efficiently).

We may also call a fee a service fee (We use the term "service" to mock you for naïvely believing we either want to or have to serve you.)

We may describe a fee as a cost recovery fee (even though we are a fully-funded, non-profit pedantocracy, i.e. non-profit in the sense of nobody benefiting from us except us).

To completely bamboozle you, we call a fee a reciprocity fee. It is beyond comprehension for most people in regular daily parlance.

When we use the word reciprocity we mean that we consider you an enemy who always loses to us.

One of our favourites is "right of landing" fee, which indicates that we consider you an aircraft and we won't let you land until you pay up.

Essentially, we can use whatever names we randomly make up at a particular moment to amuse ourselves and to take your money for none of the nonsensical excuses that we invent. People with less money are easier targets for us.

Our minds are always vacant and indifferent to the real world around us.

We took an uber taxi directly from our graduation ceremony to our office, never to see the light of day again.

We are the ultimate separatists, no longer obliged to mix with or smell the foul odour of the unwashed masses.

The fee we demand has no relationship to our actual costs. It never pays for actual services.

The proceeds of fee collection will <u>not</u> go toward hiring more staff, paying overtime, or improving and speeding up service.

Paying a fee will not result in any noticeable or unnoticeable increase in efficiency or efficacy.

That expectation is a joke, right?

The fee is by and large an arbitrary charge in token compensation to us for the inconvenience and annoyance of looking at the form you fill out.

We mean only looking at, not actually reading it.

The fee is also an arbitrary charge in token compensation to us for the inconvenience of having to file your form under miscellaneous, somewhere that we might be able to find it again.

The fee can also be assessed for some other reason which we are under no obligation to divulge to you, ever.

If you have a service complaint, don't call us, we'll call you. There are no phone numbers or e-mail addresses that you can use to reach us.

We never have to serve you because we are protected from you in a building surrounded by barbed wire, land mines, motion detectors, alarm systems, door codes, surveillance equipment, and heavily armed guards.

You will never be able to reach us.

We do, however, have a round the clock, every day, toll free automated service phone line and a website.

Press "0" at any time to talk to a live agent, if they are not all dead, sleeping, playing games on line, out shopping, on vacation, in water cooler meetings, or disconnecting the phone ringer so as not to be annoyed by it while reading a dime novel detective story or other literature with our office tablets.

We are permanently experiencing heavier than normal phone traffic, even in the middle of the night.

Your call is unimportant to us, so we don't know why you bother calling and waiting on hold indefinitely, while we play and replay the same recorded message about services we don't provide, until you go absolutely mad, angrily hang up, or die.

If anyone accidentally does answer the phone while you are waiting, if only to hang up and free the line to use it to call a food delivery number, we are sure that you will have forgotten the reason for your call by that time.

So we will thank you for calling, hang up, and note that your call was answered and your inquiry was succesfully resolved.

If you manage to engage us and remember why you are calling, we will explain to you that your inquiry cannot be handled over the phone and you should consult our website.

We will quickly add, "Is there anything else that we can do for you today?" before hanging up abruptly because your call has been cut off, by us, and we have reduced our phone volume to the point of being unable to hear you.

We won't be listening to you, in any case. Our standard question is merely rhetorical.

If you do call, always expect to wait an indeterminate amount of time for someone to answer the phone, if anyone is in the office.

In the event that you believe, in your frustration, anger, or worn down depressed state, that we are at any time actually answering any question, seek psychiatric help immediately.

We are not responsible for incorrect or misleading answers to your questions.

Visiting our website will not help you in any way whatso-ever.

Visit our site only if you wish to experience an endless loop which will always return you to the page where you start.

All you have to do to set this process in motion is to click on "contact us".

Whether you call us or visit our website, we are sure that you will be unable to receive the service that you only imagine you will receive.

If you are not satisfied with the service that we don't provide, that is a foregone conclusion.

Before lodging a complaint, we suggest that you shut up.

We don't take kindly to people who complain about us.

We consider all complainants to be whiners, malcontents, and trouble-makers. They lack our education, training, and experience in not serving the public, particularly customers.

They can never hope to understand the intricacies of our lack of work and how much effort we put into filling the empty, boring hours of each day at the office, accomplishing nothing and providing no service to anyone.

Of course we will never retaliate against you for complaining.

So go ahead. Make our day, punk.

It could be entertaining for us, if we bother to look and chuckle over the tears of frustration shed on your complaint form.

You are free to complain without fear of retaliation. Retaliating against you would take up too much of our valuable time. We would have to work at it.

Besides, there is no need for that type of unethical behaviour.

You have our guarantee that we will ignore your complaint and we will never serve you under any circumstances, whether you complain or not.

So take your best shot. The only time, energy, and effort you are wasting is your own. Always remember, we get paid to ignore you. You get paid nothing.

We'll continue to just sit back, relax, do nothing for you, and routinely collect our pay regularly and enjoy our employment benefits until we retire.

Then we'll shove off with a tidy pension.

You must always realize that nobody is going to pay you for complaining to us. Meanwhile, we will continue to get paid for not serving you.

Whether we work for the government bureaucracy or a company bureaucracy with goods and services, you will be paying our salaries.

We pay taxes and purchase company goods and services too.

So don't even try to argue that you have a right to expect service from us because you are a taxpayer or a customer.

That doesn't cut any favour with us.

By the time you're through trying to complain about us, you will become so frustrated by our lack of interest that you'll probably end up with high blood pressure leading to a stroke and/or heart disease.

Then we can simply close your file, if we ever get around to doing so. At least we'll get the last laugh, at your expense. We can dance on your grave.

Don't ever delude yourself into believing that filing a service complaint form will get you any results. We rule all forms.

Your next step will inevitably be to fill out a form to appeal our decision to ignore you.

It will end up being yet another form for us to misfile and lose, whether on paper or in electronic format.

As a final resort you may, if you are physically attractive or have a nice personality, appeal to our in-house ombudsperson.

In such cases, with physical attractiveness in particular, our most skilled personnel in the arts of assault will gladly service you. Read the Canadian play "Ten Lost Years".

But giving yourself to our staff consentually is no guarantee of receiving any service. We remain completely objective and provide everyone with equal treatment.

You will always be treated equally and exactly the same way as everyone else requiring or desiring service, i.e. nobody should ever expect service from us.

Always remember that we are not your servants and never will be. Public and customer "service" are ironic, not real.

If you exhaust all avenues of appeal, due to some physical or personality defect, you might try taking us to court, but only for cocktails or wine and cheese.

We do not accept bribes but we love to receive generous, unsolicited gifts and gratuities with no strings attached. We will always gladly string you along and not help you.

Spare no expense in your generosity and be assured that it will have no influence whatsoever on our determination not to serve you.

We are invincible and our pedantocracy is immortal.

We might be fired for stealing from our employer, if we are caught, or for intoxication at the "work" place, if any of our peers notices that we're drunk with power or otherwise addicted.

But we remain immune from punishment for incompetent public or customer service, including and not limited to the interminable and indefinite waiting periods during which time you will receive no service or information regarding when you might or might not receive service.

Always assume that you will not receive service. We will never disappoint you.

You might be dead before we decide whether or not to serve you. Your health, mortality, and longevity are of no consequence to us.

The statistics department handles such matters.

So long as you live, we will be persistent in asking you an endless number of questions until we find fault in you and your answers, and until you unwittingly provide us, out of fatigue and exhaustion, with incriminating information about you that can be used for denying you service and persecuting you in a court of law.

The "internal affairs" sections of police department bureaucracies are merely going through the motions compared with us.

If you do not fill out a form, we will punish you.

If you do fill out a form, we will punish you.

If you do nothing wrong, we will punish you.

If you fail to meet our deadlines, we will punish you. Your file will be considered complete and it will be automatically and permanently closed, never to be seen again.

We will not set any deadlines for ourselves and we will have no fear of consequences. There will be none. We have no deadlines.

We are pedantocracy. Pedantocracy is immortal.

You are a mere mortal.

You will submit.
You will be absorbed into the submissive masses.

Resistence is futile.

We always win. You always lose.

Glossary of forms

The bureaucracy's ultimate form is the form letter. A form letter sets the standard in bureaucracy non-communication.

It's the lowest possible standard.

It's like making up a false excuse for truency in the school system and absence from the job.

The form letter is a labour-saving device.

It enables bureaucracy to avoid reading all correspondence or at least to read as little as possible of it.

The underlying assumption in the form letter and in all bureaucracy non-communication is that public comments, complaints, and suggestions have no value and are best ignored altogether.

The bureaucracy has nothing to gain by reading correspondence, particulary if it comes from citizens and paying customers.

Paying attention to them is a distraction and undermines productivity in the bureaucracy.

It can also lead to mistakes, such as well-thought-out corrective action.

Actually trying to help people is a mine field that is very dangerous for bureaucracy. It can be a career changer, i.e. a lost promotion.

If anyone in bureaucracy is obliged to actually read correspondence, by some rogue elected boss, the form letter is the final resort and the last great hope for bureaucracy.

The form letter can cover almost any eventuality and all exposed tops of legs.

The form letter can be a finely tuned or very poorly written response, so long as it follows the prime rules of form letters:

Completely ignore the content of arriving correspondence.

Write about some unrelated or similar-sounding matter or about a hypothetical situation, in order to confuse the form letter's recipients.

The theory is that the recipient of the form letter will be so insulted and annoyed that s/he will throw up her/his hands and give up.

Or s/he will go off on a tangent based on the form letter and forget why s/he writes in the first place.

Either way, bureaucracy's form letter neutralizes the correspondent.

If s/he does not give up and/or go off on a tangent, the next response from bureaucracy will be one of two.

Bureaucracy will send:

i) the correspondent a duplicate of the original form letter; or:

ii) a variation of it containing the same sentences, with a few added phrases which also don't answer the correspondent.

Bureaucracy's sincere hope is that people will go away if bureaucracy writes as little as possible, and as vaguely as possible.

The form letter leaves room, (light years in fact), for misinterpretation and misunderstanding.

Thus, the bureaucracy can be held blameless.

At the time of writing, the most popular form letter phrases are the easiest to spot.

Bureaucracy has gone so far along the road to pedantocracy that it no longer perceives any need for pretense in non-communication.

If these phrases aren't obvious it means pedantocracy has triumphed.

The most innocuous form letter phrases are the most patronizing.

It is now commonplace for bureaucracy to start form letters by writing, "Thanks for reaching out".

In highly profitable, i.e. understaffed corporate bureaucracy or one using algorithms instead of human staff, the form letter will begin by saying you're getting a randomly selected form letter reply.

The computer or human sending the form letter will say that s/he's "joining the conversation".

This means the correspondent has to start writing from scratch because someone in the bureaucracy with no idea of what the correspondent is writing about wants to be brought "up to speed", i.e. 0.001 km/hr.

In political office bureaucracy there is no longer any effort to seek or retain votes by helping voters.

One of the most common form letter replies says that your letter will receive "the attention it deserves", i.e. it will be filed under miscellaneous and accidentally-on-purpose lost.

The political office bureaucracy believes that you are too stupid to comprehend the obvious insult of the word "deserves".

The bureaucracy is saying that your correspondence doesn't deserve any attention.

Another common form letter reply seems more innocuous, saying that your correspondence "has been noted".

Preposterous. At most, your name is put on a "do not reply", "trouble-maker", "enemy", or "no fly" list.

Nobody knows why you are "noted" because nobody in bureaucracy bothers to read what you write.

Bureaucracy is not saying that you are a noted author.

Wash, rest, bath, or what...

There are so many euphemisms for toilet in English, yet they all lack precision and clarity. At one point I start saying "TR" or "toilet room" to improve communication.

When I'm dealing with anyone who seems to mistakenly believe that I'm cold or unemotional, I say that I'm looking for a unit in which to deposit human biological waste products.

In a tiny Québec Ciy "hotel" near Chateau Frontenac twenty years ago, the entire room is a TR. The bed, toilet, and bath tub are all in one room.

Only a curtain divides them.

Outside and inside that room, all the words for toilet are wrong.

Washroom means a room where you wash. Restroom means a room where you rest. Bathroom is a room where you have a bath.

Yet people tell me that they go to the bathroom to take a shower. Where are they taking it?

So many bathrooms now contain only shower chambers, like some of the apartments we rent.

The most accurate, clear, and descriptive words I come up with for toilet room over the years are uritorium and defecatorium. They say it all and neutrally.

Nowhere

We are all finding ourselves always in the middle of nowhere. Nowhere is now and here.

I get surprised by a younger couple I meet at a party.

They ask me if I'm with the contra dancers. I jokingly say, "No, we're with the Sandinistas."*

(*That group over-throws Nicaragua's dictator Samosa with a U.S. churchist president's blessing.)

Looking blank, the couple says, "Who are the Sandinistas?"

Wow! The couple are small children at that point in recent history. But the Sandinista Party still runs Nicaragua.

The final irony is that a woman who emigrates here from Mexico is also at the party and brings along some samosas that she makes.

Ferme Caribou's bargain coffin

Gilbert's coffin sits on a ledge inside his barn, ready for use. It's not that he's dying or nearly dead.

He introduces it to us by saying, "Want to see my coffin?" Gilbert strings us along by saying he'll need it eventually.

It's no fatalistic resignation or a macabre joke waiting for Hallowe'en.

On a road near here, a truck full of empty coffins has an accident one day and much of the cargo gets thrown off and damaged.

The owner disposes of them at discount prices. Gilbert takes advantage of the sale.

Hot air festival

Gatineau's annual weekend Montgolfières festival seems to be all hot air. It's a hot air balloon festival, but that's not what I mean.

The event is more sound than sights from our viewpoint.

It happens in the planted over waste dump behind the adult education school right behind our place.

We see no balloons at all, at anytime, anywhere in the sky or on land as we walk in Gatineau and around Parc de la Baie, the waste dump.

All we hear is noise. All we see is a midway and garbage strewn everywhere in the streets of our neighbourhood. The balloon fest is a bust.

Movie star struck

One time my Carioca friend Zita and I are in a movie theatre and happen to encounter one of my former students from my former workplace.

She's a student at a private university here who takes English courses on the side. I have seen her in passing on that campus, riding her bicycle.

This very young woman is always particularly gentle with me in class, telling me to catch my breath and relax if I just run into the room.

When I see her at the movie theatre she looks both pleased and concerned. She says to Zita, gulping in mid-sentence: "Are you… married?"

When Zita says, "No, we're friends." the former student can hardly contain herself, beaming out in a great smile and in unconcealed tones of joy blurting out, "Oh! It's so nice to meet you!"

Zita will laugh about this story for a long time and tease me about my potential fiancée.

I don't think the pleasure of the younger woman comes from knowing that we're a happy couple instead of a married couple.

She doesn't permit this interpretation or concept to enter her marriage-brainwashed mind.

She's no doubt psychologically conditioned to be manipulated by the flowers and poetry which I don't give her.

If I were a sexual predator, I would now know my next victim.

It's sad to see women who never meet their individual, human potential because they're brought up to believe that they have no worth if they don't accept certain roles and status.

A loving friend who encourages his/her partner to reach her/his potential and to strive for the "impossible" is worth much more than a thousand husbands and wives.

Marriage ties are too often like neck ties.

They're just collars which bind and inhibit free expression of the personality and other manifestations of independent thought and intelligence.

A husband may just be someone who is there to "have and hold" back a woman. He keeps her, like a zoo keeper.

In Nippon the chains of marriage really are self-imposed by such a woman.

The marriage is virtually a dormant relationship in too many Japanese households.

The couples cannot hope to know each other during their prime physical and mental years. He's always away at work.

Of course couples who are strangers are nothing unique to Nippon.

Childcare and employment separate many couples in other parts of the world too.

Older people may find themselves living with spouses they haven't known for years or never knew at all.

Years later, my partner Mariko tells a story of such older people, as recounted by one of her Aikido martial arts colleagues.

In the true story, a woman is sitting beside her husband, who is on his death bed. He says, in nostalgic tones, that he always loves her and would marry her again.

The woman looks the other way, saying nothing.

Overcast means too many major stars appear.

When marriage isn't gay

I tell people that I'm from a mixed marriage. My parents are male and female.

Same sex marriage becomes a popular topic for discussion among many of non-gay people.

It seems about as unlikely, unpredictable, and illogical as hockey fanatics talking about golf or tennis.

Some of the non-gays say they feel very threatened by matrimony among people they don't know and don't understand, and therefore they don't like.

They don't respect gay marriage as equal access to a public and religionist services.

So why not ban marriage for everyone?

I see the civil and human rights of gay people in the same way as I see the civil and human rights of women. I'm an outsider to the direct and immediate impacts on their lives.

I don't have the right to make laws or legal decisions telling women whether or not to have abortions because I am not a woman.

I will never have to consider the possibility that I will become pregnant, go through it for nine months, experience morning sickness and labour pains, and then spend a couple of decades devoting my life to a child and then it's child or children.

From conception to birth, my body will never feel a thing.

I never have a uterus. I won't have to divert my attention away from what I want to do to monitor my pregnancy or to breast feed a new-born.

In a country with a democratically-elected government, I am free to express my opinion on anything and everything, including a woman's free choice to have or not to have a baby or an abortion.

However, I know that my views on some things, such as women's free choice, could be based on incomplete or incorrect information, especially if I don't listen to any women.

I lack the knowledge and personal experience to have a competent opinion on women's free choice.

My opinion is inevitably and unalterably weak and faulty on women's rights' to make up their own minds about matters that concern only their female bodies, not my male body.

At best, I know that I can only assess their situation as a strictly objective, outside observer.

I will never feel any direct or immediate personal consequences of my opinion if it becomes a law.

In this matter of opinion, all of the competent, informed opinions, decisions, and their consequences are the exclusive domain, jurisdiction, and prerogative of women alone.

Males who religiously take an oath of celibacy have no right whatsoever to tell women or men what they must or must not do with their bodies.

Some religionist celibates already face criminal charges for sexually abusing children. Some apparently want to abuse adult women too?

Male lawmakers and male judges don't have the competence, expertise, knowledge, or legitimate authority to make decisions on abortion on behalf of women.

All male legislators and legal practitioners should recuse themselves from all decisions governing women's bodies.

Males in these kinds of jobs should not be permitted to make laws and judgements, or vote on them, in regard to abortion and other choices under exclusive female jurisdiction.

The same argument applies to my stance on marriage. Only unmarried people have the right to decide whether or not to marry and who to marry or not to marry.

From my perspective, unmarried gay people are the same as unmarried non-gay people.

Preachers can decide on a case by case basis whether they want to preside over any particular marriage and collect the fees derived from the job.

Preachers don't have to marry any two people.

However, preachers don't have any special right to legally violate the civil and human rights of anyone.

It's up to the churches to sort out which preachers volunteer to preside over marriages when a preacher refuses to marry a particular couple or type of couple.

However, preachers who refuse to preside over gay marriages should be prohibited from presiding over non-gay marriages too.

They can abide by this rule or defrock themselves.

Refusal to marry anyone based entirely or largely on gender and sexual preference can be the beginning of more extremist actions.

Some churches could try to oblige their gay members to set up and attend segregated churches.

In the event of a referendum, would the non-gay voters permit the gay voters to set up their own churches and conduct marriages like the non-gay churches?

Or is freedom of religion, like marriage, only for non-gay people?

I don't know the church precedents for marrying couples in minority dictatorships such as the one that rules over South Africa for so many years before the country liberates itself.

Trevor Noah's book <u>Born A Crime</u> tells me that it was illegal for non-gays to marry and have children there if parents didn't have the same colour skin.

Separate but equal isn't equal. It's Apartheid.

Ron's favourite story

Mariko meets Ron during our first life in Québec City. He runs a local L.B.E. and needs someone to explain some aspects of Japanese culture to some of his students.

In the years that follow we see Ron many times when we return to this city. One particular time is so interesting for Ron that he recounts the story of it many times.

The story is about what Mariko and I call our "official marriage reception". It occurs seven years after we marry at city hall in Dazaifu, Nippon. We're not ceremonial.

My parents will arrive in Québec City for only four days and finally get to recognize that Mariko and I are together, after our 15 years together.

They also get to recognize that we're officially married, after not knowing it, and still not knowing it, for seven years.

We have an unconventional Friday the 13th mock ceremony that's really only held for my parents' benefit and for the entertainment of Mariko's parents and cousin Miyuki.

This event is only possible thanks to the help of Mariko's pals of nine years ago at l'Université Laval, Hitomi and Stephane.

They help us stage a pre-reception event by saying a few words in French and Japanese. My parents interpret this event as a wedding ceremony.

It may look like one, but it's not. Mariko and I write some words which honestly explain that this is "a day like any day", but the presentation looks ceremonial to my parents.

Hitomi and Stephane appear to be officiating when they speak Japanese and French. My parents neither understand nor speak either language.

Hitomi and Stephane are simply saying that Mariko and I are married in Nippon and we are making statements prior to the "official marriage reception" the next day.

Mariko's parents neither speak nor understand English or French. But they understand what Hitomi is saying.

Miyuki lacks the language skills to understand the English and French we're using. But she also understands Hitomi.

To ensure that our communications plan works, Hitomi and Stephane pretend that they don't understand or speak any English. They're also sworn to secrecy.

We give Hitomi a script of what she is to say in Japanese. Stephane can say anything he wishes en français. None of our family guests knows what he's saying.

Our respective parents can't compare or exchange notes. We control the interpretation. There are no other guests to tell the tale at the true statements mock ceremony.

Mariko's Nipponophile friend Michel, who is not here and remains invisible since Mariko's graduation from Laval, uses his computer to make up an official-looking document, in French only, to make my parents feel good.

We have two of our parents witness the document, which disappears forever this day. It has no legal validity and needs to be gone. There's no shred of evidence, just shred.

The reception and guests arrive the next day. We tell cousin Steve and family to come for the reception day so that they won't get confused by the ceremony.

Steve speaks and understands both French and English.

The ceremony and official reception are a good excuse to finally get my parents to visit us in Canada in the middle of winter, which they don't manage to do during all our previous times in this city. We don't arrange it then.

On reception day, most of the guests are francophones meeting each other for the first time. They include my long time friends from Donnacona and people met hitch-hiking.

Of all the guests, only Ron and his partner Denise know what we're doing linguistically.

They speak both French and English, but we ask them not to tell anyone at the reception, especially my parents, that there is no wedding or wedding reception going on.

Everyone plays their parts well and does not reveal what's actually happening. For years people tell us that they remember being at our wedding and/or reception.

During my dad's last year alive, I mention that Mariko and I are having our actual anniversary of marrying in Dazaifu. I only say that this day is our anniversary.

His memory is fading. I ask him how long he thinks Mariko and I have been married. He correctly states the exact number of years since we marry in Dazaifu.

He always knows or he is making an exceptionally lucky guess? I honestly don't know the answer to that question.

Allo!? Trop co-voiturage

Mariko and I learn about "Allo Stop" during our first year in Québec City. It's a pre-arranged and paid hitch-hiking system, but passengers have to pay.

It's much cheaper than bus, train, and plane fares and schedules are arranged to suit drivers and passengers.

Instead of standing at the roadside waiting for a ride, Allo Stop has driver and passenger members who arrange to meet at convenient spots inside the departure city.

They pay a small annual fee to belong and passengers pay only for actual rides.

Allo Stop collects a fee for each ride from the passenger and the passenger pays another small fee to the drivers. It makes the cost of the ride cheaper for both rider and driver.

Before Mariko and I leave for Paris we find out that there's a similar group there. For some reason Mariko books a ride and I don't.

But we show up together at the pick-up point in Paris, predicting that the driver won't mind taking another paying passenger.

We're right. He welcomes me. But he surprises us too.

His vehicle isn't the compact or large size that usually takes passengers out of Québec City.

He's driving a very tiny car which already has two passengers crammed aboard and hardly enough space for Mariko to sit beside them.

So we let that ride pass, losing only what Mariko pays for the reservation. The driver loses one fare too.

Bien compris

On another departure from Paris, several years later, Mariko and I manage to talk our way into two European railway passes intended for residents only.

I have a stamp in my passport saying that I can stay in one of the EU member states for "an indefinite period of time". My indefinite time rubs off on Mariko by association.

Residents can buy the passes in each member state, but the passes are only valid outside the country of purchase.

I don't quite understand this limitation and apparently neither do the people at SNCF who sell us the passes and arrange our reservations out of Paris to Amsterdam (Netherlands).

After we prepare to sleep in our compartment the night we leave Paris, the conductor arrives and asks for tickets.

When Mariko and I show him our passes and reservations he says that, strictly speaking, we can't use them for leaving Paris.

He says, "Vous comprenez?" several times while explaining the limitations of the pass system. He adds that it's all right this time, but not again.

So we get to sleep our way out of France for no extra charge.

In subsequent trips to and through France in years that follow, I find the liberality of SNCF continues, no matter what the official limitations on our tickets.

All I have to do is ask three different SNCF employees at the same train station and we will be permitted to diverge from the official rules. Génial!

Fish story at Henry's

It's warm and welcoming in a breeze ranging from light to imperceptible.

Even at the end point of the entire European peninsula, pointing to the Americas, I barely need my lightest blue sweater.

Cliff faces all around have big surf lashing on long sand zones and on rough cut under-cliff crevices.

I see the cliff scene in various places before.

The plethora of micro fauna and flora growing on the field of volcanic rocks here takes me back to the previous northern summer's sailings along Côte Nord and Labrador.

I'm also thinking of the Saga Prefecture coast near Fukuoka.

Below us are the fishers of Sagres casting their lines as far out to sea as their strength permits, using live crabs for bait and standing as far out on the cliff ledges of volcanic rock as the balls of their feet can still maintain an equilibrium, adding sargos to their bags.

One fisher shows us what he's catching and suggests we go to the nearest restaurant, just over there, for a taste of his fish. I explain that we already eat his sargos there.

At least that's what I think I'm saying to him. Then he makes the same suggestion to me and I repeat the same answer.

As we walk away I wonder why we aren't able to communicate well in Portuguese. Then Mariko explains what's happening.

I'm mixing Portuguese and Japanese words, using taberu instead of comer.

I think I'm saying, "We already ate it." in Portuguese, but I'm combining the two languages by saying "Jà tabemos."

The result is incomprehensible in both languages.

What's left makes right?

It seems strange for people with rights to vote for or against extending rights to people without rights.

There are no referendums to create or write the major civil and human rights documents now considered norms and standards in the G8 and associate states.

When only males can vote in referendums, do they vote to enable women to vote?

Do Euro-faces in the U.S. and South Africa vote in referendums to end Apartheid segregation against non-Euro faces?

Between two lakes and one bag

After an overnight stay in Winnipeg we leave late in the morning, heading north on Highway 6, putting on my Australian sun screen between rides to Ashern

That's a journey of only a couple of hundred kilometres.

The town campground includes a huge statue of a chicken, much to Mariko's chagrin. She finds the scene exceedingly foul.

The Ashern chicken is bigger than I can estimate, in any measure system. I only know that it dwarfs my 188 cm. height by at least double.

Gulls perch on its head, saying "Mommy" in gull talk?

Perhaps the enormous bawker without baulk is also responsible for keeping bears away from our camp ground.

I see no trace of the forest heavies. We bundle up in the tent to keep out the colder than expected air, not in fear of invisible bears.

We do have a sleeping bag, yes only one. We try to use it as a ground sheet inside the plastic floor of our plastic tent.

When I get chilly during the night, I pull both Mariko and the sleeping bag over my back. I sleep very well but she doesn't.

This becomes our story of Mariko's experience as a human sleeping bag.

The next day we discover more evidence that the few locals visible between Winnipeg and Thompson must hold birds in high esteem.

Lundar has a Canada Goose in its municipal flag, alongside a red maple leaf. Lundar also has a giant goose weather vane swinging in the wind on highway 6.

The goose is smaller than Ashern's chicken. Diet?

Reigning over cats and dogs

On the home front, I lose a lot of sleep during our first four months in Miyazaki because of one yappy neighbourhood dog. Its master leaves it out all night.

It stops barking just before midnight and starts again at dawn. When it wakes up between those times, it barks some more. So it is a source of sleep deprivation torture.

Finally, Mariko gets the local government to convince the owner to keep the dog indoors, at least all night.

I use guerilla tactics to get some other dog owners to follow suit.

If a dog barks in the middle of the night, I get up, walk over to the offending master's house, ring the doorbell, and politely speak into the intercom in Nihongo.

I say, "Good morning. It's 3 a.m. Your dog is barking." The problem is solved forever.

It's a house-by-house battle, but I win.

Mariko helps me avoid the late night walking by noting the names of dog owners on name placks outside their homes. Then she looks them up in the phone book.

That way, I only have to phone them if their dog wakes me up. It's a form of reciprocity that works.

For strays and sneaky people who let their dogs run lose and bark randomly at night, I first try running after the noise makers and throwing stones to drive them away.

When that fails I dispose of the problem in the same last resort manner as I deal with stray cats. It's a secret approach that catches them by surprise.

After I solve the existing dog problems, a new neighbour buys a dog that barks non-stop whenever it's put outdoors, day or night.

It yaps desperately and pathetically toward the sliding door of its master's house, begging to be let inside.

Even when the neighbours are home they don't seem to hear the noise until we complain, along with many other neighbours.

I release the poor mutt when it disrupts one of our classes. It's so happy that it affectionately runs after me, jumping on me and licking my feet.

Finally someone is paying attention to the poor creature.

But the dog just goes home and barks again when I run back to class.

Mariko writes a polite note asking the offending dog owners to have pity on our students, even though we captivate them so much that at least they don't hear the dog.

She also complains to the local government, the police, a new police mediation hotline, and the traditional neighbourhood association chiefs.

During one dog barking fit, I go to visit each neighbour, all retired people in large homes, point out the problem, and say that the poor dog is barking and no one pays any attention to it.

The barking noise is all over our home too.

The neighbours are very sympathetic. One of the older male neighbours goes to the dog's masters and offers to take care of the dog when the owners are out.

But the dog owners just ignore the senior citizen instead of respecting him in the traditional Japanese manner and accepting the offer the way that a polite local person normally would do.

The offending neighbours finally keep their pet indoors at night, but they continue to abandon it outdoors during the daytime, especially during our classes and when we want to have quiet enjoyment, record materials, or watch videos.

I decide to let the poor dog free again. It wanders around the neighbourhood all day getting wet in a small rain storm.

That night after our last class, the neighbours come running up our stairs and start yelling at us about letting out their "child", as they call it.

I can't agree more with the unintended insult to themselves.

The woman of the couple on our doorstep threatens to punch me, Mariko tells me later.

My ignorance of the language they use means that I only understand the violence of their voice tones and facial expressions toward us.

They are definitely not truly Japanese. They only look it.

Finally, a few minutes later the police finally come to talk to us. But it's not because of our many complaints, which they <u>are</u> sympathetic about.

They laugh when Mariko goes to their neighbourhood police office and tells them we're letting out the poor dog.

The police finally come to our door only because the neighbours accuse me of going into their land and letting their dog loose.

The police, who never come to see the situation until the dog owners complain, soon realize that the dog is kept on a tiny strip of concrete between the house and the road.

That's "their land".

Obviously, I don't have to trespass to let the dog free. But the police have to advise me not to touch the neighbour's property, including the dog.

When we go to the police station to ask why they come for the dog owner's complaint but not for ours, they try to assure us that they don't intend it to appear that way.

They say that the law enables them to respond to physical trespass complaints but not to sonic trespass complaints. Noise by-laws cover planes and traffic but not dogs.

The police, the government, and everyone else we complain to become very happy for us when the bad neighbours suddenly pack up and move out of our neighbourhood.

They have to move only because they're unwilling or too lazy to just care for their dog and to train it to respect the neighbours.

Cats are another matter. No one has jurisdiction over them. The government won't touch them because they might just be house pets running around.

Mariko thinks a lot of the cats are abandoned by apartment dwellers who move away.

She says that people get dogs and cats when they're cute puppies and kittens. But when they grow out of that stage the owners lose almost all interest in the pets.

When we first arrive in the neighbourhood there must be twenty cats in every stage of sexual overheat, growling around our building all day and night.

I feed them some strange-tasting cat food. After that there's only one cat per year. The strays probably perish or change their dining habits.

Maybe the house cats are treated for a mysterious stomach epidemic and kept indoors.

Few return. They must be house pets with great resistance to strange food. The cat-astrophe is over.

Mariko and I are pet vigilantes who help the neighbour-hood sleep more soundly.

...Mariko spends hours single-handedly solving this prob-lem, along with noisy motor cycles in the night, cars leav-ing engines running outside our windows, carelessly dump-ed and messy garbage, etc.

She says that this is the first place she ever lives in Nippon where she ever has to complain to the police and city hall.

So she calls Miyazaki a "nuisance city". (Mariko lives in at least five different places in Nippon.)

Chance origins

Is the outport of Come-by-chance in Newfoundland & Labrador, named due to its functionality or lack thereof, or a variable fertility rate that's influencing birthing frequen-cy?

It's your baby now

Since Mariko is always with me at Kamata's dental clinic, the communication is clear and precise.

It also means that she's always talking to the dental clinic people and getting to know them.

It becomes a very pleasant experience for all of us. The clinic people like us so much that they take extra pictures of all our teeth and give them to us.

They also want us to pose in group photos with them. We become stars in the promotional video that they make and show on the TV in their small waiting room.

One cute and tiny dental hygienist becomes so friendly with me that she takes me aside one day and ushers me over to the secluded entrance area when no one else is around.

She tells me in soft tones, with her usual happy smile, that she's pregnant.

It's very nice of her to confide in me. I feel as if she considers me a very special friend and that pleases me. She's so nice.

But the context is funny since we have no sexual contact.

An outside observer witnessing her secretly telling me that she's pregnant might conclude that she's talking to the father.

When I tell this story to Mariko I joke about it, saying, "What's that have to do with me?" But at heart I still feel privileged and touched by my friend.

Catalogue
(perfect writing with clause)

(This humour only scratches the surface.)

syndicate: faulty or flawed

catastrophy: posterior award

cattle: mispronunciation

cataract: risqué biting stage play

catamaran: unusually fond of water

caterpillar: scratching post or prescription drug

cat house: everywhere

catsup: giving something a licking

ketchup: pause finally reach

catnip: slight injury

Cataluniya: homeland

Catskills: résumé item

catalyst: for only the best category; horror film

catalytic converter: impossible

Catalina: good diet

Katmandu: Do you?

catscan: Can you? includes pause button

Katarina: small coliseum

catching: more Chinese coin

catbird: error

catboat: liquiphobic

catbrier: curly hair

cat burglar: kidnapper; or larcenous

catch: sneeze

Catch 22: severe allergy

catch-all: epidemic

catcher: mewrah!

catchy: martial art using four legs

catechetical: censored

catechism: Where's my food!?

catechize: Feed me now!

catecholamine: reverberating sound

cat ice: U.S. border guard

cateran: flight

cat walk: no vehicle

catgut: courage

cathead: perfect rule

cat face: realistic

cat fish: swipe and bite

catenary: old calendar

catiline: waiting room at vet's

caterwaul: to keep out dogs

Cat and...

Computers makers who encourage people to finger screens or type everything out are trying to discourage cats from becoming customers. That's the game.

Candy store capers

First a correction: These tales are about a neighbourhood grocer, i.e. a shop owned by a person having no connection to a supermarket or "convenience" chain.

But for those of us who are frequent consumers of bubble gum cards with baseball players on them, pop, fugicles, popsicles, Crackerjacks, animal crackers, and whatever else is primarily a non-nutritious, low cost sugar hit, the grocer is a candy store merchant.

Purveyors of sugar are the only legal kiddy drug lords in our neighbourhood.

We're six year olds with some of our parents' income to dispose of in unwise and self-injuring ways.

We pay for the ill effects of sugary treats on our teeth with painful drilling and filling work in the dentist's chair and our parents pay the dentistry bills for the sugar's damage.

Our cravings for a sweet taste in our mouths can go to the extremes associated with hard core addicts.

One day in front of the candy store, a shopper drops a bag of groceries on the concrete sidewalk out front. "My apple juice!" she exclaims, as liquid pours onto the sidewalk.

Yes, liquids come in glass bottles at that time.

I'm on the sidewalk at that exact moment and see one of the other kids dropping to the ground and starting to lick up the "apple juice".

How unsanitary! He's nuts! I'm not thinking of the nutritional value of apples.

Only when he starts lapping up the "juice" does the shopper cry out that there's a now broken bottle of bleach in her bag is also.

The kid soon vomits up the juice and bleach cocktail. I later hear that he'll be all right and I see him walking around.

The other candy store incident involves me personally and makes me a local celebrity, for a while.

I come into some money. Someone in my family gives me 50 cents. It's a fortune in a candy store where one cent can buy more than a single item.

I put it all on the counter and ask the candy pusher for the equivalent in jawbreakers. They're a hard round, multilayer candy that changes colour as you lick off each layer.

Eating jawbreakers is about more than tasting sugar. It's about taking the jawbreaker out of your mouth and looking at the changing colours.

These candies are probably called jawbreakers because if you bight into one you'll surely break your teeth, if not your jaw bone.

Every cent I pay gives me three jawbreakers. So I have a fortune in the orbs. I literally have a 50 cent bag with 150 jawbreaers in it. It's a life's supply?

Of course I share them with every kid standing on the sidewalk out front. The swarm grows around me.

Lots of little fingers in various stages of grubbiness, moist-ness, and stickiness are thrusting themselves into my open paper bag to rustle out one or two jawbreakers.

Suddenly I'm the most popular kid on the corner.

But my generosity, benevolence, fame, and popularity are short lived.

My mom comes home from work, sees the contents of my bag, confiscates it, and goes after the candy shop owner.

She says that she lays into the candy pusher, telling him that he's irresponsible to take so much money from a kid just to sell candy.

I don't know whether the merchant gives all the money back to my mom and resells the leftover jawbreakers in the bag.

But after that calamity, even if I make one of my normally small candy purchases, the merchant always asks me, as a condition of sale, if I'm sure it's okay with my mother,.

No Souvenirs

Mariko tells me that as a child she's small enough to fit into a futon closet. So that's where she likes to sleep. She finds it warm and comfortable. There she has other dreams too.

She takes action to fulfill at least one of them.

When Mariko and her schoolmates go on organized bus trips to various places as part of the school curriculum, there's always a stop at a souvenir shop along the way.

Parents give their children spending money. All the kids pile off the bus and buy something with their coins. But not Mariko.

She gets 100 yen. Instead of buying anything, including 300 jawbreakers, Mariko saves the 100 yen that she receives.

She's so determined to keep it for an important purchase that she's the only school child who won't even get off the bus when it stops at a souvenir shop.

She keeps holding on to her 100 yen souvenir spending money until it accumulates to a substantial sum. Then she uses it all to buy what she really wants.
It's a bed.

The environmental mess is my fault.

Before my birth, my parents go everywhere by public transit, bicycle, or on foot. After I arrive, they buy a car that pollutes the air.

Then I demand tooth-rotting candy and gut-destroying snacks.

So millions of hectares of productive, fertile land become manufacturing plants for junk food and its packaging.

I cry loudly for every kind of defective hazardous toy on the market and so cause the misuse of tonnes of natural resources.

I waste megawatts of electricity for nearly two decades by watching TV and playing records.

I deplete the supply of non-renewable fossil fuels by purchasing hundreds of plastic records.

So I oblige governments to build nuclear power stations and that makes me responsible for the accidents at Chernobyl and Three Mile Island.

I use more fossil fuels to glue and paint scale plastic models of hot rods, planes, and spacecraft. The old glue I use is also toxic and addictive.

While the paint is drying, I'm reading science fiction.

It convinces me that I don't have to do anything about exhaust fumes because polluting cars would vanish before I reach my twenties.

So I'm guilty of environmental negligence too.

I'm also a repeat offender when I see the beautiful Canadian Rockies national parks towns being destroyed and I do nothing about it.

The first coating of pavement is replacing the old dirt and gravel roads that keep out the squeamish and their precious unscratched car exteriors.

The first battalions of tour buses, recreation vehicles, and cars are coming over the horizons to invade the pristine wilderness and drive out the wildlife.

The construction gangs are pouring a deluge of asphalt over the gravel and dirt streets of Banff and Jasper.

The luxury condominiums and their parking lots are spreading, consuming every hectare of greenery between the mountains and rivers.

But I do nothing and I'm sorry.

I'm so grossly negligent and destructive toward the environment because I'm caught up in my daily routines, fads, and fantasies.

I'm living without thinking and without taking any action.

I expect big corporations, governments, future generations, and some automatically evolving better world to solve all the environmental problems that I cause.

I'm wrong.

Now that I've confessed to creating the environmental mess, could we please all start cleaning it up?

We each have to ask ourselves:

What am I doing every day that's harming the natural environment?

(I have to stop doing it, right now.)

Which ordinary, natural experiences am I enjoying now that I want to last for generations?

(I have to continue these experiences by practicing them very often.)

What do I want to preserve in the environment right now while I still can?

(If I don't preserve it now, it will be gone forever.)

Thorny province

Alberta governments aren't very resourceful. They depend entirely on drilling holes in the ground. The holes render the land unfertile.

In the past they at least put something into the ground that grew and nourished people.

Now they try to use all their energy to end human life on earth. Now only debt and poverty grow in Alberta.

Alberta's governments have holes in their heads.

The province also has too many holy rollers. They're playing craps beyond blind belief. They gamble on the invisible and reject what they can see, like compulsives.

In Alberta and far beyond, most of the people who dig holes in the ground are lucky to get paid minimum wage.

Cross ride

Some places in the world, I see Christianists making a cross sign over their chests every time they walk past a church.

Such devoted behaviour helps me to understand the origins of the word crosswalk.

But the sidewalks aren't the only places where I come across public crossings.

I'm observing the same intersection of movement and religionism whenever I'm aboard a public transit bus passing in front of a church.

These vehicles must be cross town buses.

Segregation

I have my first segregation experience at the bus stops of Córdoba, Argentina during the military dictatorship years.

Males and females line up separately and females board first. This must be a token gesture of respectful behaviour for the otherwise domineering macho males ruling females.

I smirk at the sexist spectacle, not knowing whether I should laugh or cry.

I don't see the same thing in later visits to this city. Good.

Going Beyond Idle Talk

Every time the city bus stops for a red light, the driver turns off the engine. When the light turns green, the driver turns on the engine again.

Some mechanics tell me this is not good for the engine. But not leaving the engine running is good for the environment.

Idling motors spew out tonnes of air pollutants.

The bus driver is making the right choice. He must be a new driver, still a young activist making a statement and setting an example. He hasn't gone cynical or sold out.

No. He probably has twenty-five years driving experience and a bit of white hair.

Turning off the engine at red lights is actually company policy.

It must be a publicly owned transit system, or a new company with a new, enlightened CEO, using his power to make a difference and improve the world.

No. This is a private company that has been around for a long time. CEOs have come and gone.

They are typically older, experienced business men who have relatively conservative outlooks. The engine off policy continues regardless of who is in charge.

It is a policy that's more than 30 years old.

So this story is about Sweden or some city with very tough environmental bylaws created by a popular council elected to clean up the city.

No, it's Fukuoka, Japan, a fairly small city by Japanese standards that has been growing into a little Tokyo during the past two decades.

Nobody in my circle of Japanese friends seems to know exactly when or why the bus drivers started turning off their engines during red lights.

My friends don't remember a time when the drivers didn't turn off the engines.

But somewhere along the way, some people reached a consensus and made a choice. That's how things are supposed to work in Japan.

The choice was in favour of the environment instead of the engine.

Unfortunately, the same choice has not yet been made in most Japanese cities.

In a much smaller city about 400 kilometres from Fukuoka, my casual observations find just the opposite attitude, by at least some drivers, toward leaving engines idling.

Here's my report on random daily observations in a grassy parking lot:

* One of my neighbours just bought a large shiny red sports car. But he rarely drives it. Usually, he just cleans and polishes it.

His car is his temple.

So when he sets out to drive, he dons very clean looking ceremonial blue overalls and a racing cap before gently easing himself into the hallowed driver's seat.

He trembles in anticipation as the engine revs. Everyone within a 20-metre radius trembles in my neighbourhood.

It's a long revering moment while the devout driver goes into a trance, mesmerized by vibrations in the bucket seat.

Silent prayers for peace begin, as people all around the neighbourhood beg for a miracle, the car's rapid departure.

As we despair, after all hope of tranquility is lost, the driver is ready to roll. He pulls out of the parking spot.

But then he stops again, in mid-parking lot.

He is scrupulously honouring the sacred law against using a cell phone while driving.

It's time to call his friends and let them hear the engine roar.

He chats for an eternity. Then he's suddenly gone. But quicker than you can say "Thank goodness it's quiet again," it's the second coming.

The car returns, expelling hell and brimstone, spewing out big, dark exhaust fumes. Then it shuts down.

Is this car worship really worth the cost to the air and sound environment?

* Another neighbour uses a huge, eight-passenger van to commute all alone.

Every morning he slides in, starts the engine, and pulls out his electric razor. The bathroom at home, across the street, is occupied?

Couldn't he get up earlier and shave off some toxic emissions time?

* A nearby company worker gets into his smaller van, turns on the motor, and reads a book. He uses the overhead light after sunset.

He needs time alone to relieve his stress before going home?

Why not seek refuge outside the car, where his personal relief isn't putting more stress on the clean air supply?

* A tiny sports car convertible backs in slightly faster than a truck. The exhaust pipe is aimed at the open windows of the neighbour's house.

The motor keeps running, providing musical accompaniment, while the driver slowly peels off his patent leather racing gloves, and gently opens the door.

It's a dramatic entrance, worthy of James Bond.

But that's not him.

Out pops some middle-aged man with dark-rimmed glasses, and short, neatly cut hair, wearing a very conservative business suit and a grey tie.

It's a public transit fashion statement.

Why burn all that fuel to park such an ordinary appearance?

All these drivers could help reduce air pollution by thinking about what they are doing automatically, just as automatically as they turn the ignition and let the motor run.

The key to cleaner air is in every driver's hand.

Gentlemen!... Please Turn Off Your Engines!

Autos

Is a person named Otto deemed Ottonomous?

Is a magnet attached to a metal car chassis autocollant?

Authenticating educational toys

In the early deluge of Noel television advertising following immediately after Hallowe'en, I notice a baby doll selling that enables children to feed it with plastic food, which is probably as nutritious as the junk food that other commercials are selling the real children.

In the past I have only seen dolls which are flexible, close their eyes, walk awkwardly, play back recorded phrases, record and repeat phrases, and drink water.

From the artificial vision of the latest innovation, I begin getting inspired about designing realistic, educational children's toys.

I start by joking that the dolls in the commercial should also urinate and defecate so that the children can get the complete baby feeding experience.

Later, I think they baby doll should become obese when it is feed too much.

Finally, I realize the potential of this approach to toy making.

By intent or not, toy doll makers are stimulating, contributing to, and feeding on parental instincts in humans still in the process of developing physically, mentally, and emotionally.

Toy doll makers are meddling in human instincts by creating products which simulate only some of the parenting experience.

Unfortunately, in so doing, the toy doll makers are also misrepresenting that experience, contributing to false, misleading, and totally unrealistic impressions and expectations of how it feels to live with and care for a real human baby and child.

So I suggest making the toy dolls more realistic, to help children experience a life-like simulation of parenting and child-raising.

I suggest the toy makers create a product called "real doll".

The real doll will be a cute robot with a soft, smooth shell, and hair that grows on the bald head it starts with before it is activated.

According to the real doll user agreement, which all owners must submit to without exception:

Once activated the real doll cannot be turned off, day or night. Not ever. The battery charge lasts the entire child owner's life, until s/he dies holding the real doll's hand.

The real doll only functions when the child who owns it is located within a certain radius of the doll, which means a distance roughly equivalent to the size of an apartment, condominium, or house and property.

In other words, it's within audible crying and screaming distance.

To extend that distance, a real doll monitor is connected to loud speakers both indoors and outdoors.

All the real doll owner's communications devices and computers are connected to the real doll monitor too.

The child owner may be required to undergo chip implant surgery to ensure user privacy, i.e. so that only the owner will be rendered disturbed by her/his real doll.

The real doll will automatically calculate the perimeters of its sensors and detect the child owner everywhere therein.

If the child owning the real doll goes beyond the household sensor radius of the real doll, the tracking function is activated.

It's somewhat like an extended version of house arrest.

If the child owner strays too far from the real doll, the authorities are automatically notified and issue a real-doll-neglect-warrant.

There is nowhere to hide from the real doll.

The real doll will also be attuned to respond only to the child owning it, through biometric scanning of the child owner when the doll is purchased, new or second-hand.

The second-hand purchase is only legal if the first owner dies prematurely from caring for the real doll.

The functions of the real doll are as authentic as technologically possible, with updates and upgrades as technologies change or improve.

The real doll with duplicate and simulate every aspect of a real human baby and small child's behaviours during its first two years of life.

It will lie, then crawl, and eventually learn to walk and talk. It will grow in size according to its care and nourishment.

More specifically, the real doll will have to be fed liquids, then solids. It will then soil its diapers, which have to be changed and cleaned.

The real doll will not accept disposable diapers. Of course this means the real doll needs to be fed and changed at regular intervals.

The real doll is programmed to inform its child owner when it requires feeding and changing. This will occur at random intervals both day and night.

For this purpose, the real doll comes equipped with a voice alarm, audible only to its child owner.

The voice alarm will also notify the child owner of the real doll's "status" at approximately two hour intervals.

During the night, the real doll voice alarm will always sound whenever the real doll sensors detect REM sleep in the child owner.

Voice alarms will vary from simple crying to intense, loud screaming.

When the real doll develops word skills, the voice alarms will repeat phrases such as:

"I'm thirsty! Get me a drink! I'm hungry! How about some food! I want it now!   Wake up and get to work! Help!"

Upon delivery of the ordered order, real doll will say:

"I don't like it! Yuk! No! Why do you serve me this swill?!"

Very soon after only partially consuming the liquid or solid nourishment, real doll will cry out:

"My diaper is full of urine and feces. It really stinks! I'm becoming a bio-hazard! I tore it off! Now everything is covered with urine and feces, including me. Hurry up!"

The slightest delay in clean-up will cause real doll to shout very loudly:

"What kind of a parent are you? Come on! Right now! Step on it or I'll contact child services and have you arrested!"

The phrases become more advanced as the real doll develops higher mind functions. Eventually real doll will scream, "I hate you!" and slam doors very loudly.

Real doll would be the most advanced and honest educational toy ever invented, enabling children to realistically evaluate the whole baby and early childhood care and nurturing experience.

Thus, as parental instincts grow while children become adolescents and young adults, potential parents who learn from real doll will be very well informed and prepared to decide whether or not they wish to follow their parental instincts into parenthood.

The probability of a baby boom would be greatly reduced. The threat of a worldwide population explosion would finally be put to an end.

Real doll would also contribute to preventing accidental, unintended pregnancies, births, and potential cases of child neglect and abuse.

Some adolescents and young adults might conclude that childcare is an experience similar to the most frightening scenes from teenage horror movies.

Real doll would be an ideal gift for any and every young child. Both males and females should have a real doll.

More advanced real doll models could be developed to accompany children as they grow up, so they can also experience later child-rearing experiences.

These real dolls would grow to become real adolescent dolls, reaching a maximum age of 16, and remaining that age forever.

Growing children owners of real adolescent dolls would be financially and legally responsible for these dolls, which could move independently almost anywhere and do almost anything, always displaying the name of their young owner.

For parents who want to make their children safer, stronger, and tougher, ready to meet any challenges in life without fear, I suggest creating another type of realistic, educational doll.

It's called soldier doll. It would have all the biometric scanning and operating parameters of the real doll, plus even more capabilities and accessories.

Soldier doll would give every child, male and female, the "boot camp" experience, every day of his/her childhood and adolescence.

A child and adolescent owner of soldier doll would be awakened every morning well before dawn and given their orders for the day.

Along with the usual household chores and schooling of a routine childhood, the child owner of soldier doll would have a regime of vigorous physical exercise under the ever-watching eye of solder doll.

It would bark out orders loudly, in aggressive tones, with appropriate insults when it sensed the child owner was not cooperating and not functioning at full potential.

Any disobedience or recalcitrance would mean soldier doll's proximity to its owner would become nose-length. Soldier doll's voice volume and insults would become louder and more severe.

The more the resistance sensed, the more soldier doll would become aggressive and forceful. It would never take "No.", "I'm tired." or, "Leave me alone." for an answer.

Soldier doll would provide full military training, including war exercises and games.

For safety reasons, only soldier doll would be provided with real weapons and live ammunition.

By the time a child grows from childhood and adolescence to full adulthood, s/he would be able to behave like a fully trained and competent soldier, baring accidental maiming, crippling, or death from soldier doll's "friendly fire" or related psychological disorders such as "shell shock".

This educational toy would also enable children and adolescents to alter the soldier doll's programme, override and cancel it, if and only if the child owner makes full and thorough use of another educational toy, which s/he has to build, rebuild, and operate him/herself, every day, forever.

It's called the "democratic society doll". Only it can demobilize, deactivate, and render harmless the soldier doll.

When I allude to some of my "real doll" ideas to friends Louis-Paul, Isabel, and their now walking baby daughter, Isabelle says "On ne veut pas ça"

While they're going home Louis-Paul mentions that he needs so much energy for their child that he's too tired to work when he gets to the office in the morning.

I say people should have children when they're 15 or 16 years old. Louis-Paul and Isabel say that's a good idea because people that young are full of energy.

They suggest that 13 or 14 might be even better.

I tell them I agree and say it's a very good idea because the teen parent's parents still have to support their kids and pay for everything.

Mariko can hardly contain her laughter.

Futons?

There's nowhere I'd rather sleep than in an authentic bedroom of Nippon or Hangoo. That's because there's no bed.

The room is empty all day. The room can be used for anything all day and only becomes a sleeping place at night, just before sleeping time.

No bed is taking up floor space, preventing me from making full use of most of the room, and creating more cleaning work by collecting dust underneath the bed.

Without a bed I can also have a comfortable sleep at night.

I sleep between two authentic futons. I mean real futons that are full of light, fluffy, soft cotton that easily fold ups and fits in a closet, out of sight and out of the way all day.

It's not some awkward heavy chunk of furniture that's always dictating a very limited version of usable space.

Don't be fooled and lulled to sleep by fake futons. Don't lie down for imitations.

Look beyond the distorted dreams of European-implanted U.S. world views. A futon is not part of a French verb conjugation.

A futon isn't the stiffened and softened version of a mattress posing as a futon in Canadian shops. A futon isn't a Danish quilt, a comforter, a blanket, or a sleeping bag.

A futon is soft and pliable, yet firm and solid. It is creaseless, seamless, unsectioned. It's sewn together, not buttoned down.

It's smooth, not lumpy or bumpy, and it's never saggy. A futon is meant for a special floor, a tatami mat in Nippon.

Futons are more challenging and complicated than the pale comparison counterfeits absconding with the name abroad.

Futons aren't for the lazy or over-stressed who never make a bed and routinely leave it in a mess.

Futons are much more demanding than making hospital corners with sheets and blankets. Futons need daily, careful folding.

They have covers which have to be peeled off, washed, and slipped back on. Futons need regular sunning and fresh airing to make them clean and wonderfully fluffy places to dream in.

My attempts to slip the cover back on and my efforts to attach futon corners with strings or buttons is quite a struggle.

I'm having difficulty subduing the futons into a flatness matching their covers, length to length and width to width instead of the contrary, width to length, before finally zipping up this work.

My efforts make Mariko laugh.

Makie factor

This story has some basis in fact and real life. It's true that Makie teaches her husband Steve how to make up a futon for sleeping.

It's also true that there is a certain way of putting extra blankets on top of a futon and under a futon during the coldest season.

Each blanket has a label in one corner on one side. The label is supposed to be placed a certain way, face up at the foot of the futon.

The practical reason for this is so that the same part of the blanket will always be on the feet and the other part will always be over the shoulders, instead of switching back and forth at random.

People apparently don't like to mix their feet and their shoulders.

When Mariko and I go to visit this couple one time and stay overnight, Makie is out of town for a few days. So Steve tells us what he learns about futon blankets.

He adds that if he put the blankets on the wrong way, "Makie would kill me."

During a later visit Makie says she's not that strict anymore, and her former severity is just the way she's brought up.

But the image is already in my mind.

So quite often I tell Mariko, when we're putting down the futons in winter, that we'd better be careful because Makie will "kill" us we if we get it wrong.

This is where my imagination kicks in to make Mariko laugh.

The story begins one night while we're spreading out the futons. I jokingly remark that we'd better put them out correctly or Makie will kill us.

But I'm careless and put them out wrong.

No sooner do the futons settle to the floor when, all at once, the phone rings and there's a loud, thudding knock at the door.

We answer the phone first. It's Steve, all in a panic. "Don't open the door!" he shouts. "It's Makie! I warned you!"

We quickly rearrange the futons into their right juxtapositions, and then go to the door. No one is there. Phew!

Tech stress/tough love

Popular mythology, created by computer software companies, describes computer screens as if they were some kind of magical windows or openings helping people both near and far away to communicate and to get closer than possible to each other.

In this neo-reality, the windows break down inhibitions and other forms of shyness and the windows overcome large geographic spaces in between computer users.

One drop out from the educational institutions who turns a motor vehicle garage into a lucrative computer business, and in the process becomes someone with more money than brains, calls this phenomenon "the miracle of the Internet".

In the real world, however, the greatest barrier between any two people is a computer screen.

The magic windows are more like sorcerers who put people into trances, taking their full attention away from everyone and everything in the immediate surroundings and the whole living world of nature and humanity around the computer user.

In offices where people once have no alternative but to see and look at each other, i.e. their co-workers, the scene is now obscured by a maze of screens on desks, blocking views of all around.

Workers can only see virtual reality instead of actual reality.

This reflects upon all their work and its effects on humanity, making the office and its relationship with people inside and outside more remote, out-of-touch, and lacking in truly human contact than all past bureaucracy.

It's a sure fire work system for manufacturing defective products and descending into very poor customer service plagued with dictatorial attitudes and behaviours.

An inhuman office is the worst form of ruin and bankruptcy.

The eye strain, muscular malfunctions, and pains received from screen sitting and staring, and the great pains taken to keep the screens fluid instead of frozen, add to already stressful employment.

This creates an environment of grumpy, irritable, short-tempered screen slaves.

The screens make people jumpier than the chronic caffeine addiction which once has the exclusive role of stirring up anxiety and tensions in employment.

In homes where affectionate-feeling people formerly live as lovers and true couples, spending years gazing lovingly into each other's eyes, there are now only two virtual strangers.

Pining romance is no longer the source of their suffering.

They now endure only an electronic variety of tunnel vision, like horses wearing blinders preventing them from seeing anything that is not straight ahead.

In this case, wearing blinders means having only an un-blinking, glazed over, dull stare pointing directly at and only at the object of all emotionless obsessions, the computer screen.

Screens now turn a younger person's once adoring, longing, yearning looks into blank and agitated stares.

Love cannot be unrequited when there's no love to requite.

The humans have quit each other and nobody's missing them. What's to miss?

Jealously is extinct. Raging emotions are directed elsewhere. All love is reserved for the screen.

Anyone disturbing this devoted loveless relationship with a computer, by interrupting screen concentration, is going to get a glare, not an affectionate stare, and then an angry shout to all interlopers, "Go away!"

Erotic encounters are dead. They're only simulated in cyber space.

All the sighing, heavy breathing, gasping, moaning, and murmuring go only to inanimate partners in the void now.

All the crying out, in anguish more than pleasure, is devoted entirely to frigid keyboards, lifeless screens, and lost data.

They alone can stir up emotions and frustrate their human partners.

Whispering sweet nothings is futile.

Sweet nothings are now rendered inaudible by the intermittent bursts of repeated tunes, beeps, and tones.

Sweet nothings are now drowned out by the unmusical accompaniment of a recurring whirring sound made by the motor of the computer cooling fan.

Perhaps no human in all eternity ever receives the undivided attention that users now shower upon the inanimates we call computers.

Users are devoting entire lifetimes, from childhood to biological death, almost entirely and exclusively to the screens.

The computers' human love slaves are putting house pets and parents to shame in their unconditional love and absolute loyalty.

The oldest, most happily together, never parting couples of legend and yore could never in their wildest dreams have any hope of claiming or achieving the ultimate fidelity of the user to his/her dearly and truly beloved, lifeless, emotionless computer screen.

It's the most amazing, loveless true love story of all time, a tale of passionless passion.

Computer users pass many more long nights together and many more long years of repeated intimate tactile contact together than any human couple could ever hope to achieve.

The staying power is unequalled, i.e. the power of staying in one place, in front of the screen.

Even the mere concepts of separating or divorce are unimaginable. The computer and the user belonging to it are inseparable.

They are the most perfect couple of all time.

This relationship is completely free of all the human couples' necessities and foibles.

In the truly extraordinary, impersonal relationship between a computer and its user, there is no need for love potions, perfumes, or other cosmetics.

There is no call for body-building or a wonderfully varied and stylish wardrobe, or sexy apparel.

Nor is there any necessity for cosmetic surgery to hold this odd couple together.

In this exceptionally blind love, a world darker than a black hole, users are attracted only by a lifeless flat screen, not shapely contours or voluptuous curves with a vivacious interior.

There is no seducing at all. There is no alluring, philandering. Nor is there any two-timing. Cheating is gone forever.

The user doesn't need any of that. The user turns compromising into a completely one-sided matter where s/he does all the compromising of his/her life to maximize computer access time.

The user is so self-effacing in her/his relationship with the computer that s/he makes a person behaving like a door mat to his/her human partner look egotistical.

No power surge or outage, no crash can keep this loveless loving couple apart for long.

Nothing can stifle or extinguish their eternal partnership, until in the user's death do they part.

There will be upgrading and new generations of operating systems, software, and hardware, but this couple will still be giving each other the same intent blank looks until the user battery expires and s/he is recycled as land fill or incinerated to ashes.

The chastity and devotion of the users in this lifelong, selfless, sexless love affair is so total and unyielding that it might be cited to put in question the sincerity and commitment of all monks and nuns in all their human-deity relationships.

Unconventional cloisture

If nuns can live in a nunnery, why can't monks live in a monkery?

Mariko and I walk past just such a cloistured enclave in the lower part of Vieux Québec. It has fortified gates and at least one round-shaped insecurity camera.

Aren't people living in such enclaves supposed to have an absolute faith that their extraterrestrial superhuman is always watching over and protecting them?

So why the earthly protection? "Oh yee of little faith"?

Caged

They're held within a chicken-wired enclosure, tiny tots hardly old enough to walk.

Some stand at the edge, clinging to the wire and gaping into the distance for any sign of rescue. They seem to be in hypnotic trances.

We try to catch their distant gaze by smiling and waving, but they ignore us. We are invisible to their yearning minds.

We pass this sad scene every day. Only once do we see one of the litle children bouncing on its knees and grimacing in frustration. They usually stare patiently.

Is this a detainment centre set up by the U.S. government to confine children separated from their economic refugee parents?

No. It's an outdoor enclosure outside a daycare near central Québec City. Children are patiently and impatiently waiting to be picked up by their parents in the late afternoon.

Chaotic vote results?

Since there are municipal elections everywhere in Québec this year, after a fixed term of office of four years, I get to hear one story that's even stranger than the Montréal election.

During the TV news the day after the elections, I find out voters in Magog choose mayhem on election day.

Yes, the voters choose mayhem, I mean May Ham, Vicki May Ham. Nobody seems to get the joke because it's in English?

Judeo-nasties?

Conventional news reports say that there are "right wing Israeli nationalists". They march through the streets shouting, "Death To Arabs!"

It's the nationalists' "final solution" throughout time?

These nationalists can't be the descendants of victims of The Holocaust.

The Yahoo running Israel supports invading Palestinian land, turfing out the residents, and building what the United Nations calls "illegal" settlements.

It's a re-run of the European 500 year rampage around the world, except for the fact that the U.N. wasn't around then to declare Europe's invasions and occupations illegal.

The territory in question, bordering Israel, was voluntarily ceded to the Palestinians by a now deceased ruler of Jordan.

But Israel, particularly under Yahoo, decides to just confiscate the land and anex it for Israel.

Israel needs, as the nasties in Deutschland said, living space.

The latest episode in this humanitarian tragedy involves Israeli's evicting Palestinians from their houses, reminding me of the nasties taking over the homes of Polish Jews in the U.S. Holywood movie "Schindler's List".

This has to be a very bad joke. It can't be serious.

Semantic couple

Ignore and ignorance are an undesirable ideal match.

Menu write-off

I write these sentences for my partner Mariko because when I am very inspired or otherwise working on a writing project, I give it my complete attention, ignoring all else:

I prepare a scrumptious banquet of words that can nourish the world for generations to come.

In so doing, I neglect to prepare the food we need to live.

Vegetarians are immune from pork barrel politics and poultry bribes.

I'm invited into homes for dinners and attend community meals as well.

At one point in history, which I hope is long past, I make some significant observations.

At all of these eating events, the female people do all the food preparation work while their male counterparts stay far away or at most arrange the table or tables and chairs.

When the women bring out the meal and eating is about to begin, the men then insist on saying a prayer with words that "Thank God." for the meal.

Shouldn't they be thanking the goddesses who do all the work? Or are the prayers outlandish jokes? Women don't have a prayer?

Masquing reality

During the COVID-19 world pandemic, wearing a mask to cover most of the face is a safety requirement for everyone out and about.

Thus I can write:

All the world's a masquerade party and none of us can board the stage to go beyond.

This writing is not universally true or practiced.

It's amazing how many people look so young and attractive, until they take off their masks.

Rent all

A skate boarder pays no rent.

Be it ever so unknown, there's no place like nowhere

I can honestly say that I'm from nowhere and feel no particular attachment to the place of my birth – neighbourhood, city, province, or nation-state.

My parents move me around so much, starting at barely age 6. I live in so many different neighbourhoods and go to several different schools.

We are not being sought by the police, although my mom often says that my childhood playmates in our first neighbourhood probably all end up in jail.

When I become an adult I'm well prepared to want to live everywhere that I'm not from. So I do that, across Canada and far beyond it.

Within Canada I'm sometimes blamed for the deeds of the most recent of my addresses.

I'm decried as a Québecker and a Westerner. One anglo-Montréalais insists, "You're a French-Canadian." When I try to explain that I truly am not he says, "Yes you are!"

Living in a particular place at a particular time means I have no choice or voice in defining my own identity?

In theory, being from nowhere should always get me off the hook and save me from being blamed for the ill-deeds of people who actually are from somewhere.

That's the best reason for being from nowhere. Once I explain myself, nobody can blame me for what those other people are doing wrong.

It must be difficult to go through life being attacked for the location of one's accident of birth.

When people ask me, "Where are you from." The easiest answer is, "That's a long story." I can also give my other pat answer, "Most recently or originally?"

But, as I discover, that can be asking for trouble, as I already mentioned.

The other complication is that they start asking questions or making comments about my place of birth. I can only smile and nod about that place I don't really know.

Besides, when they make the choice I'm giving them I can only explain that my answer doesn't mean anything.

I hardly know where I'm born and I stay almost everywhere else for only a short time. I'm uninformed and clueless.

Bishopland

After a few years absence from Québec City I notice that a major thoroughfare changes its name, as another main street does in downtown Montréal.

Both are now named for René Levesque, who is Québec's premier for nine years.

Maurice Duplessis is premier for about 18 years. Jean Lesage is premier for six years. Robert Bourassa is premer for about 15 years.

There is no major street that I know of in Montréal or Québec City named for any of those other premiers. Why?

I understand why Duplessis is not placed on any major street. His reign is known as "le grand noiceur".

He collaborates with churchist leaders as they do with the U.K. occupation U.K. colonial rulers holding back Québec for nearly centuries.

I'm not sure about Bourassa.

His lack of political courage blocks Pierre Trudeau from passing The Victoria Charter, the first Canadian constitution authored and controlled exclusively by Canada and replacing the U.K. parliament's B.N.A. Act.

Bourassa is probably best known for building a large hydro-electric power plant at James Bay.

Although Lesage ranks with the shortest two of the four-premiers, he liberates Québec from the Duplessis era and accelerates "la révolution tranquille".

This makes Lesage the most significant premier in modern Québec history. Without that revolution there could be no Bourassa or Lévesque.

Lesage makes television reporter, interviewer, and commentator René Lévesque the cabinet minister responsible for creating Hydro Québec.

So Lesage is Levesque's mentor in politics and government.

But only Lévesque is immortalized in changed major street names in Montréal, Québec, and probably smaller centres too.

Why?

Lévesque creates a hard core separatist movement and unites the divided separatist parties of his time.

That grouping separates into divided parties again only in much more recent years.

But Lévesque's separatist goal is overwhelmingly rejected by Québeckers. He loses a separatist referendum to Pierre Trudeau and Jean Chrétien by 60% to 40%.

Fifteen years later another premier loses another referendum by barely one per cent. Why are the streets not named after him instead of Lévesque?

I only find one very short, obscure back street named for that more successful referendum premier, near l'Assemblé-nationale. He doesn't merit a long major street?

Essentially, Lévesque supporters loved him and idolized him the mythical proportions. In their eyes nobody else merits major streets named after them.

Arguing against naming streets after Levesque could be perceived as negative thinking and opposition to the rights Quebecois(es) gain under Jean Lesage.

The street renamings cause me to have mischievous thoughts about honouring Lévesque.

Why stop at naming only two major streets. Rename everything Lévesque.

Streets can be numbered from Lévesque One east and west as well as north and south to infinity.

All Métro de Montréal and Québec City bus stops can be named and numbered in similar fashion. Every ligne of the Métro can be ligne René Lévesque with a colour code.

Place d'Youville here in Québec City can be renamed Place Lévesque. Youville was just a nun and a slave owner to boot.

All place can be renamed accordingly.

This would outdo Argentina with its Placa San Martin in every city and town.

La Musée des beaux arts, La Musée de la civilisation, and all the others can have the name Lévesque at the end too.

Every sports arena, stadium, airport, and train station can be renamed for Lévesque too.

All churches can be renamed l'église, le cathédrale, or l'oratoire Saint René Lévesque. Forget about Papal approval and all the other clergy.

René comes first among l'évêque.

Like others gaining unconditional love, deification, idolification, and mythological stature, René Lévesque is a religionism held in reverance among his most devout admirers and followers.

Of course highways 20, 40, and all the rest must be renamed too. Just call them e.g. L'autoroute Lévesque 20, etc.

Every ministry of the provincial government can be renamed for Lévesque, e.g. la Lévesque ministère de la santé.

Political parties should be renamed. The first ones to change their names should be Le Bloc René Lévesque and Le Parti René Lévesque, both can be abbreviated to René Lévesquists.

Québec Solidaire should be renamed René Lévesque Solidaire.

Hydro Québec should be renamed Hydro René Lévesque.

Vidéotron, Bell, and all the rest need to be renamed Communications René Lévesque.

Why settle for merely renaming places, routes, ministries, corporations, and buildings?

Poutine, tarte au sucre, and sirop d'érable should be re-dubbed René Lévesque patates, tarte au René Lévesque, and sirop de René Levesque.

Gilles Vigneault and Céline Dion should be required by law to change their names to René Lévesque and Renée Lévesque. Artists of all types should follow suit.

In this way, all works of art, including performing arts, can be attributed to René Lévesque.

Come to think of it, why limit the renaming to all of the above? Montréal and Québec should be renamed Lévesque too, Lévesque Ville and Ville de Lévesque respectively.

Trois Rivières should be Trois René Lévesques, the holy trinity. Not to be outdone, Sept Îles should be Sept René Lévesques. Why should he be restricted to only a trinity?

Le fleuve Saint Laurent should be called le fleuve René Lévesque. Les laurentides ought to be les René Levésques.

Finally Québec should change its name to René Lévesque.

After all, Québec is an Algonquian word, not French. So the language law (101) should not permit the word Québec to be prominently displayed in public sineage.

Renaming Québec Lévesque would solve that problem.

Ulitimately, Québec can never be truly libre and have full sovereignty until everything is renamed René Lévesque.

René Lévesque Libre is the only way that René Lévesquers(euses) can be truly free and advance.

Everyone will finally be able to proudly declare:

"Je suis René Lévesquer(euse)!"

Funny names

When I'm 16 and come to Donnacona for the first time, I notice small cartoon joke books in French selling in a local store.

On the cover I see the word "Québecois" for the first time.

I ask Édouard what it means. He says, "It's a funny name that we call people living in Québec."

Three years later, in St. John's, Newfoundland & Labrador, I see itentical-looking cartoon joke books with the word "Newfy" on them.

Much later I learn more about the word Québecois in its historical context.

When people from France arrive on the east coast of Canada, they name the place "Canada" and call the First Nations inhabitants "Canadien".

Later on, the French settlers are called "Canadien" by both France and the U.K.

When the U.S. colonists from the U.K. break away from their motherland, some colonists decide they prefer to remain colonials and thus move to the land of the "Canadien".

Apart from the multilingual First Nations, the arrival of U.S. anglophones makes Canada bilingual in two European languages. Up until then, the only anglophones in Canada are the U.K. occupation forces and colonial office elite.

After Canada gains partial independence from the U.K., anglophones in Canada begin to call themselves Canadians, leaving francophones with the name French-Canadians.

Anglomaniacs thereafter take such pains to impose linguistic apartheid on francophones inhabiting Canada for hundreds of years that they become alienated.

Faced with an anglomaniac seige beyond the diminishing territory of northern New France, the francophone begin calling themselves only Québecois in Québec.

Other Canadian francophones come up with different names, including the traditional and original Acadien(ne)s, along with Franco-Ontarien(ne)s, Franco-Columbien(ne)s, Fransaskois(es), FrancoManitobain(e)s, etc.

THE END?

At least one funeral business I encounter is so obsessed with concealing doctor's death certificates from the deceased's family that I'm beginning to suspect the business might be a murder suspect attempting to hide evidence of foul play.

It's a prepaid funeral business with no COD* delivery service. (*Cause Of Death).

At least some people find it reassuring and comforting to feel that there is something beyond a brain behind our eyes.

The concept of having a soul helps many to hope that aging and death are just temporary states of being with something better to follow.

But what post-life can be more amazing and spectacular than a supernova star we call "The Sun" splitting us all into infinitesimally small particles that are scattered by the ensuing black hole to everywhere beyond trillions of light years into every micro-nanometre of cosmic space?

Who would choose, instead, to be stuck in the same old never-changing "paradise" with the same old dead people for an eternity?

The whole idea having to co-exist with churchists in their "life everlasting" makes me cringe.

Spending an afterlife with a bunch of virgins is no more appealing.

They don't know what to do with you when you get there and when they do learn it might become as boring as the results of legalizing pornography on Swedish television.

As for Nirvana – It's like walking along an endless highway to a destination you can neither see nor reach, while hitch-hiking backwards along the way.

Forget about aging and death. Just live.

Beginnings

A gestation period is newly born.

Gestation: 1. prior to knowing which one; 2. temporary housing; 3. comedy radio frequency.

A greeting card tells humourous stories at every encounter.

Temporal distortion

A time zone is the only place where time can exist.

Maritime is AST, ADT, NST, NDT, and should be PST and PDT too.

Tune down

Sound tracks are stored in theme attics. They're also audible under snowshoes and boots.

A job offer to work as a prima dona is a great operatunity.

Compositions aren't always melodic or harmonious.

Do composers write M.O.?

Are printers composers?

Micropublishers hire fortune cookie writers.

Poultry facts

Profane describes an amateur of poultry linguistics.

Mikoyan i Gurevich

Even crossing our eyes Mariko and I have difficulty reading the tiny instruction sheet for completing the "partly-assembled" 1/144 scale model. Who will be able to notice?

Diminutive Convocation

At my first university graduation, the bell tower plays a song that I buy shortly before graduating. I'm very surprised to be in a procession serenaded by "Rhapsody In Blue".

Years later, I'm awakened from this dreamy scene.

Our students tell us they have to reschedule their classes because they have to attend their childrens' graduation ceremonies.

Most of the students giving us this news are in their 20s and 30s. So they give birth during or before their teens?

How can the grad ceremony organizers distinguish between the parents and their children?

Wrong. For those of us who associate graduation only with senior secondary school and universities, there is considerable confusion.

It seems that for at least the past quarter century, the word graduation has been redefined, just like campus.

Computer technology companies now call their offices a "campus". Elementary schools use the same word for their buildings.

If everywhere is now a campus, what is a university?

Graduation now applies to merely passing from one type of schooling to the other, i.e. from elementary to secondary school. There is no elementary school degree earned.

The U.S.ers talk of getting a "high school diploma". I graduated from a senior secondary school but I have never seen or received a diploma for that achievement.

Writing résumés must be more challenging now. Year of graduation is no longer so easy to declare. A twelve year old is now a graduate.

There's more to it, or less to it as well. Children completing pre-school have graduation ceremonies too. Fortunately I'm not invited. I would be laughing too much.

If pre-schoolers "graduate" does that make elementary school an advanced level of education?

I mistakenly believe this is a product of kyoiku mama in Nippon.

Then I see a U.S. P.B.S. Newshour report showing tiny tots in cap and gown walking in a procession to celebrate their pre-school "graduation" ceremony.

In my infancy, pre-school goes by the very unpretentious name of "play school". It's informally organized fun, not an academic programme to determine lifetimes.

I'm either a drop out or expelled from "play school". I never list that "education" in a résumé, but it won't render me unemployable.

Unlike me, generations of pre-school graduates will soon happily reveal themselves, saying:

"Let me show you my first diploma. No one in my family ever had this distinction before me. They were so proud. I graduated when I was only six years old."

Making the most minor events and accomplishments of a lifetime into grand ceremonial occasions tends to cheapen and under-rate all that follows. Is this the intention?

Do office walls now proudly display the framed pre-school diplomas of their senior staff?

Do professors, professionals, and executives now boast about their PsDs (Pre-school Degrees).

Do these members of the elite now compare pre-school experiences at elite cocktail parties, galas, and fundraisers?

"Oh, did you study under Ms. Smith, the exceptionally gifted 21-year-old pre-school professor?

My corporate managerment system is modelled on Ms. Smith's approach to pre-schoolers, particularly in regard to employeed relations and negotiations with unions."

Are there prestigious, C.P.D.S.* institutions? (*Centres for Post-Diaper Studies)

Is graduating from "the right" C.P.D.S. programme the new criterion for promotions, career path advancement, and being accepted at "the club"?

Graduates of "M.G.P.P." C.P.D.S. receive first preference? That's "Maple Grove Pre-Primary", if you must ask.

Is C.P.D.S. status the first entry in the biographies of the most newly moneyed and famous. e.g.:

"After successfully earning a PsD at a prestigious dandelion league C.P.D.S. with an impressive academic record, completing a combined major in crayon management, plasticine design, and creative fingerpainting, the graduate's learned professors knew that their young protégé was destined for greatness."

Grain of truth

Mariko and I become regular consumers of "whole grain", especially "whole wheat" and genmai rice. In my case it's carrying on a "brown bread" tradition begun by my dad.

I learn at a very young age that the healthiest use for a slice of white bread is to roll it in the palm of your hand, compress it into a ball, and then thrown out a window.

Suddenly Mariko turns our whole grain consumption into a joke, saying, "Are other products half grain?"

I add that some are "half wheat". What's the other half?

In a Dauphin farmer's market a home bread baker says that her whole wheat bread is "healthy bread". "So the other bread is unhealthy?" I ask.

Then she says, "The whiter the bread, the quicker you're dead."

Supermarkets sell non-whole-wheat bread that includes "enriched flour", which means that having taken all the nutrition out of whole grains to make white bread, bakers are obliged to artificially put nutrients back into the whitened flour.

Talking to Mariko, we agree that "enriched' bread may be poor nutrition but it isn't for unmoneyed people, even if this poor quality product is marketed to that segment of the population.

The moneyed owners of bakery factories are the onely ones who are truly enriched by selling the lower nutrition product.

Originally, whole wheat must be poor bread, i.e. for the unmoneyed who don't have "refined" bread needs or tastes.

The "refined" moneyed people of that era or geography are more likely to eat "refined" food. It's a slow suicide diet of highly processed food.

The unmoneyed become more vulnerable to processed food sold by companies owned by the moneyed.

That elite group devours all the natural ingredients and whole grains in order to "refine" them and sell it to the unmoneyed as "food".

The U.S. adds to the confusion by offering wheat bread and brown bread.

All breads made with wheat flour are wheat bread, including white, enriched, and whole grain bread. Brown bread only indicates that there is probably brown food colouring.

Feeding time...

Mariko and I joke when we're hungry by saying, "It's feeding time at the zoo." We usually eat when we're hungry instead of attaching ourselves to a rigid routine.

In the streets of le Vieux Québec one day we walk past one

of the many busy restaurants, often with people waiting outside in the mornings.

A group of older-looking people, even chronologically younger and similar-aged people look old to us, slows down in our path.

Up until this moment, they seem to be on their way to continuing a walk. Then one looks at his watch, remarking the time with surprise.

"Oh it's lunch time." he says, en français. The little group immediately turns and walks our way, toward the small waiting line outside the eatery we only just pass.

I can't help laughing and the joke continues for at least the next few days as I look at my watch and tell Mariko that we have to eat because of time.

I'm thinking that this "eating time" phenomenon is a sure sign that we're in the "first" world. It's a place where most people only eat when it's "time".

In most of the rest of the world that I know about, people eat because they're hungry and need nourishment.

For most people in the "outside" world, eating is a necessity of life. Eating isn't just a scheduled activity, i.e. something one does like clockwork.

Most of the world population is not fed up with time.

What's for lunch? Nashi.

Z walk

When spring brings warmer temperatures and brilliant sunshine to our neighbourhood in Québec City, the almost iceless and snowless roads and sidewalks fill with throngs.

There are always cyclists, runners, and walkers in winter along rue Père Marquette, even in the snow.

But now there are so many people walking in the middle of the street that I feel like an extra in a zombie movie.

And the moral is?

Some advocates claiming to be "pro-life" make death threats against medical doctors and commit murder.

This unsavoury behaviour is widely reported by mainstream news networks.

...

During one of my stays in Ottawa I see an older man who comes to parliament hill every day to hold up an anti-abortion sign.

Give that man a hormone treatment and a sex change operation.

Rejuvinate him and throw in a good supply of fertility drugs. Add a demanding career or serious financial difficulties.

Municipal humour

In a busy Sawaraku supermarket, I often smile at cashiers I know and tell them sympathetically that I realize they're busy.

Walking away from just such a brief encounter with a friendly cashier I think I should say, "This is Fukuoka-shi but this store is Isoga-shi."

I'm also thinking that a city where older and oppressed married women live could be called "Oishi". I'm not thinking of Atwood's Edible Woman, but I could be.

Honestly

During my first years in university, I recall some students and writers equating employment with prostituting oneself.

When I to go Osaka for L.B.E.* training one of the other participants describes L.B.E. work as linguistic prostitution. (*L.B.E. stands for the language business establishments misnomered "schools".)

But only today, to my knowledge do a group of employeed people gain official union recognition, certification, and membership for openly calling themselves prostitutes.

Now called sex trade workers, prostitutes join the Canadian Union of Public Employees (CUPE).

When will ministries of sex trade be established?

Will the newly unionized public servants become part of the pedantocracy, like the elitist, aloof, non-communicative, disinterested bureaucrats?

Terminal

What's the difference and similarity between employers and cannons?

Difference: Cannons only fire balls.

Similarity: Employers bowl over lives and livelihoods. It can be the end of the line for victims. They can become flat broke and dead.

Yard work

A landowner invites someone with experience and good references to an interviewer.

Question: If you get this job there'll be a lot of weeding.
Answer: Sorry, I can't weed.
Question: Why?
Answer: I'm iwiterate.

Out of context

The previous humour shows the importance of context for setting up a joke. Humour takes advantage of the thought-less assumptions of a reader or audience.

Ignorance, conventions, prejudices, and myths take up so much space in the minds of so many people that they are setting themselves up for unexpected and "surprising" turns in joke-telling and the humour writing often* preceding it.

They're also setting themselves up for "surprising" consequences that are much worse than not getting jokes and being perceived as people without a sense of humour, such as dying of COVID-19 in a hospital and finding themselves on a planet without a human life support system.

(*I write "often" because my own jokes are often said spontaneously before I write them down, making them more effective and sometimes impressing the listeners.)

Writing some oral jokes is challenging because the humour only works due to the sounds of words rather than the words themselves when written out.

I find this particularly true when I try to joke in Nihongo using words normally appearing as kanji in written form. Each kanji is distinct and doesn't lend itself to my puns.

I ignore this barrier to humour and make only myself laugh.

Perhaps someone with complete mastery of kanji can effectively write puns. The closest actual example that I know appears on a side street in Miyazaki.

Someone writes "gomi" in kanji, which is widely understood to mean garbage. The writer uses kanji pronounced the same way as "gomi" but which means "preserve the beautiful".

I know this is not intended to be a joke. It's simply making something unattractive look better. In effect it's also a pro-environment statement.

Waste is not beaurtiful. Not producing waste helps to preserve natural things in their beautiful state.

If we don't comply with the realities of nature, only nature will be around to have the last laugh.

Wakefulness & emptiness

If a person can be wide awake, can others be narrow awake?

The latter would be somnambulists and people with a standard issues existence mind set, i.e. asleep to reality.
Being fast asleep and slow awake can be hazardous.

Unbelieveable

Tempura is considered "Japanese food", but it's a cultural import from Portugal.

George Vancouver is considered an "English sea captain", but his family's name is originally Van Coverden and he's an immigrant to the U.K. from the Netherlands.

Names such as Diefenbaker and Gretsky are immortalized as heros of "Western Canada" against "the east". Both of these "westerners" are from Ontario.

Symbolism

Crucifixion has no counterpart. There is no cruci-non-fix-ion.

Crucifixion apparently originates in the militaristic empire of Rome*, (* a relatively minor territorial empire compared with the Chuang Hwa to Arabia empire of the Mongol Khans).

Like other empires, Rome's specialized in slaughter and conquest using massive military armed forces to crush all resistance to its rule and dominion.

Like other empires, Rome's celebrated violent, bloodthirsty sports entertainment resulting in crippling injuries, maiming, brain damage, psychological stress, and death.

The empire of Rome punished lawbreakers and dissidents by hanging them on large crosses to inflict excruciating pain and death.

So why would the Christianists choose to immortalize the violent excesses of Rome's empire by adopting the empire's torture and death construct as the symbol of the Christianist religionism?

What other religionism(s) adopts a symbol of torture and execution as it's own?   I know of none.

There is no religionism, except a pro-execution sect, who would be likely to use a hanging rope noose, a guillotine, an electric chair, lethal injection valves, etc. as religious symbols.

Even the most bloodthursty Crusaders and Conquistadores, and the most sadistic Inquisitionist torturers of Christianism don't cause that religionism to adopt swords, daggers, arrows, axes, and torture chamber equipment as Christianist symbols.

Of course adopting such implements of evil would not be out of character for that religionism.

Very Rough draft

Unfortunately, I meet missionaries in various places, including Nippon, Pinochet's Chile, and Miette Hot Springs, Alberta.

In Nippon I'm impressed by one group of missionaries because its members seem to be fluent in Nihongo.

The group also has a reputation for learning the languages
of their destinations well before going there.

Bravo for the pre-arrival language learning, but too bad for
the locals who have to listen to churchist propaganda that's
well pronounced and grammaticallycorrect.

Always ready to learn about how others learn and teach
languages effectively, I ask one of the missionaries how
they acquire their good language skills.

Her reply is disappointing. She says that she attributes her
language learning to "God" Cringe.

Is that the acronym for an educational institution in a language that I don't know?

Or is it the superhero identity of some extraterrestrial teacher?

Several years later, I hear something even more elusive and
evasive.

A churchist opponent of health precautions and COVID-19
vaccinations is saying to a news reporter that she's protected "by Jesus' blood".

Quick! Inject everyone with it! Buy churchist snake oil
shares?

The same group of missionaries who I meet in Nippon-
boasts, at their Pacific islands theme park, that they make
people more loyal to the ruler wherever they go.

No wonder they're allowed into Chile by General Pinochet's nasty military dictatorship.

I find these missionaries hiding in a movie theatre when they and I see the police going after street merchants without legal permits.

The merchants take refuge in a rival church, not the missionaries' temple.

Fortunately, the missionaires I meet at Miette are low key and they do Mariko and me a big favour when we leave the hot springs.

But the serious religionist talk, mannerisms, and male supremacy relationship of the different sexes couple are too big a target for me to resist.

In a moment of inevitable levity, I tell them that when God creates man She says, "Oh dear! What a mess!" Then She creates woman and declares, "Phew! That's much better!"

It's the difference between a rough and final draft. Even God learns from Her mistake.

Omitted in error or divine dementia

During my first solo trans-Canada trip from the west to east coast, I see the fossilized remains of dinosaurs in Alberta's Dinosaur Provincial Park.

I see other remains of dinosaurs in various museums in different parts of the world.

Scientists find huge numbers of dinosaur remains and calculate that the dinosaurs are planet earth's dominant form of life for tens of millions of years.

Yet no religionism's "holy" book that I know of makes any mention of the very long dinosaur era of earth and the universe. It's a huge missing chapter for a "holy" book.

This significant and substantial omission makes all religious wri-tings suspect.

Why would the principal documents of all religions not mention the long-lasting and most dominant "creation" of all eternity?

Does the omission have divine origins?

The supreme extraterrestrial being came down with Alzheimer's disease more than 5,000 years ago or a million years ago, and now resides in a celestial nursing home where his son "never visits"?

Nor do the "holy" books make any reference to the existence of extraterrestrials, apart from "god" or "gods" and "angels", too many of whom seem to have been created in the image of "man" rather than vice versa.

The image of woman is rarer. Has that history been erased by male supremacists everywhere?

If all the religionist books are taken at face value, they must conclude that there is no life in the universe beyond earth. That belief is definitely a fanatical fundamentalist one.

What happens when we find life on the surface or under-ground on other celestial bodies? What happens when we find life within and under ice on other orbs?

The "holy" books will have to be revised, sent back to the perfect author for an update rewrite?

Direct line spin

If some churchomaniac confronts me in front of one of his/her buildings, I'm ready to respond.

When s/he asks if I'm going to church, I can reply, "No need." When s/he asks why, I can respond, "Speed dial."

When s/he says, "Speed dial?" I can say, "Sure. I have your deity's direct line number on speed dial. Whenever I need something I just push a button."

"Are you interested in selling this deserted building? It's could be a great location for a condo-shopping complex."

Sin full

Canadian adults must be very bad people.

They always have a SIN, carry it around with them, keep it in a safe place, and show it every time they apply for some-thing involving money.

Collections division:
Disorderly misconduct

When I frequent Singapura's national library, it's about the size of a Canadian neighbourhood library, but not as well organized.

Card catalogue microfiche and books are not arranged in order.

I decide to put the microfiche in order. It takes a long time. Then I look for some interesting books. I note the call numbers.

But when I look in the shelves the books are all mixed up. To find what I want I would have to re-shelve all the books in the library.

So I just randomly look around and pick up some titles which seem interesting.

Having shelved many books part-time as a student, at UBC Main Library and at the provincial parliamentary library at Queen's Park in Toronto, I know that organizing books and putting microfiche catalogues in their correct order requires only basic literacy, not a library science degree.

So I wonder what's causing the organizational problems at Singapura's national library. The facility is useless for all practical purposes. How can anyone find anything here?

How can anyone learn even basic information if s/he can never hope to locate a book in the nation-state's main public library?

How can Singapura's lofty, modern, commercial structures hope to survive without the foundation of a knowledgeable citizenry?

Or does business and commercial success require no literacy or knowledge beyond writing numbers in a ledger book?

Galactic hazards

A locally-written science-fiction book which I miraculously find at the Singapura national library, but only once, both gains and loses my attention rapidly.

Han May writes the story, <u>Star Sapphire</u>, five years before I find it in the library. It's about a woman in outer space.

At first I think it's writing in the spirit of sexual equality but that tone leaves the book in the early pages, when the lead character reveals that she's conventional at heart despite her aspirations.

Reading the revelation is disappointing. I just leave the book on the table and walk away from it, never to see it again. Only the earliest pages are so promising.

May's first page has a good quote referring to her grandmother's death in bed. This event echoes what my dad often says to me, "Most people die in bed."

May writes that all her ancestors die in bed while living on earth, so being in bed on earth is the most dangerous place in the universe.

I can only add: So try to stay awake and alert at all times throughout your lifetime.

Victim

When Russian Federation President Vladimir Putin invades Ukraine, N.A.T.O. members are the first to cry foul.

Putin claims that he's forced to invade Ukraine because N.A.T.O., a Cold War relic established to counter the

C.C.C.P. military, is aggressively expanding up to the Federation's borders.

The C.C.C.P. was considered a "communist" enemy, but the Russian Federation is a friendly, capitalist nation-state providing oil and gas to the major N.A.T.O. member states.

The dancing comedian who becomes the elected president of Ukraine denounces the Federation, declaring Putin a "war criminal" and calling upon N.A.T.O. and the rest of the world to take up arms against the Federation.

The president forgets that such a war is the nuclear holocaut that threatened humanity during about 40 years of Cold War?

Unfortunately, he's not just kidding.

Ukraine's entertainer president wants to produce a spectacular finale for human life on earth?

The ultimate irony of this conflict is that a chorus of nation-states condemn the Russian Federation for "war crimes" and "crimes against humanity", while the U.S. still refuses to sign a treaty that would oblige its military personnel to submit to the jurisdiction of an international war crimes treaty and tribunal.

Wounded Knee, Hiroshima, Nagasaki, Dresden, Potsdam, My Lai, and Abu Ghraib are not war crimes or crimes against humanity?

Is this a very bad sick joke?

Off track betting

I wager that no one who lives through a war actually believes in total victory. War is a wager that no wager can win.

Everyone waging war loses. Military triumph when war ends is a shallow victory in name alone. The human costs of war are immediate and everlasting for all belligerents.
No war is just, rightful, glorious, valorous, or romantic.

All the war dead are murder victims. All the wounded are assault victims. All military personnel in combat are murderers and assailants.

Killing, torturing, assaulting, looting, maiming, mentally destabilizing, rendering homeless, and causing people to suffer anguish and grief far from the battlefields are not just, rightful, glorious, or valourous.

They are war crimes against humanity.

If you unleash the dogs of war they will run home and bite you to death.

VOLUMES FROM MYTHBREAKER

Terrian Journals series:

A Sketch of Terrian History
Terrian Journals' How To Make The Nation
500 Years In Louis Bourbon's Few Hectares
Full Employment: Not Fulfilling
Terrian
Terrian Journals: Living as a Newcomer
Middle Earth Journals
Rediscovery Journals
Fukurokuju No Kasumi Journals
Sabbatical Journals
Departure Journals
Adventuredate Unknown Journals
Away Team Journals
Searching For South Journals
Inonakanokawazu Journals
КАЗАНЬ Journals
Exile Journals
Tenjin Journals
Terrian Journals for the Misguided
Terrian Journals' N.S.R.: Not Spying, ...Really!
TJ JNG: Terrian Journals' Jokes Nobody Gets
Terrian Journals' Half Serious
Terrian Journals' Disbelief
Terrian Journals' House Trap
Terrian Journals' Virtually Camping
Terrian Journals' Crystal
Virtually Dead
Terrian Journals' Maximum Insecurity
Terrian Journals' Mandarinas
Terrian Journals' Living With Lords
Terrian Journals First Anthology
Terrian Journals Second Anthology

Pre-Terrian Journals:

Explorations Of Inner & Outer Space
Out of Context
Terrian Journals Origins

Archway series:

Archway: Six Year Book of Dreams
Archway: Lifetime Rhyme
Archway's Valentine Love
Archway's Garden Rhymes
Archway's Christmas New Years Rhymes

Additional Titles:

Language Learning Secrets
Trying To Teach Languages In The L.B.E. World
An Adult Book About Education
Terrian Journals' Miss Schooling?

www.ingramcontent.com/pod-product-compliance
Lightning Source LLC
Chambersburg PA
CBHW060012050426

42448CB00012B/2711